The films of Laurel & Hardy

WHAT WAS THE FILM WHEN..? has been written to provide a no nonsense pocket guide to the films of Laurel and Hardy. This format has been adopted from the 1996 A5 version. The publishers of this book will also donate a sum of money from every copy sold to the Laurel and Hardy Statue Appeal Fund and also future related events, charities and causes.

Our thanks go out to Sir Norman Wisdom OBE for kindly writing the foreword. To Bram Reijnhoudt (Perfect Day Tent, Amsterdam) and to Del Kempster (The Live Ghost Tent, London) who provided the vast majority of pictures for this publication. To Dave Wyatt who checked through the solo film titles. Also to Glenn Mitchell and Tony Marks for their proof reading skills. To Rob Lewis (Helpmates Tent) who provided several good ideas for the book, and finally to all the "Sons of the Desert" who encouraged, contributed and generally helped into making this book possible.

Mark Anthony Potts and David Shephard © 2001

Dedicated to Bill Cubin
'a good "Son" and friend'

Foreword

I am happy to say that I met Stan Laurel and Oliver Hardy in 1952 when I was appearing in a stage show in Brussels. It was after the show that something happened that was almost impossible to believe. I was told the great Laurel and Hardy had watched the show and wanted to come into my dressing room to meet me. It was so unbelievable that I thought it was a joke, until suddenly they both appeared and I almost cried with excitement.

I wondered why they were in Brussels at all at that time, but they then told me that they were appearing in the same theatre the following week. Happily I stayed in Brussels for the extra day to watch them perform and then met them again afterwards and told them how wonderful they were.

It was only a little later that we were together on a Variety Theatrical Tour in England and later performed with them in a Charity Show at the Victoria Palace Theatre in London. We became good friends. So much so that I even visited them at their homes when I was working in Hollywood, and we kept in touch for years.

Showbusiness is like that, in fact 100% is absolutely wonderful, and I'm a lucky little devil to be in it!

Norman Wisdom.

Sir Norman Wisdom OBE with Stan and Ollie, the caption at the top reads
'I was very proud to meet them both.'
(courtesy of A. J. Marriot)

Contents

Foreword 5
Preface 7
Introduction 8
Short Film Guide 15
Cameras Roll, Action - The Silent Films 25
Any Nuts? - The Talking Pictures 77
Their Final Reel - Great Guns to Atoll K 181
The Finishing Touch(es) 199
The Solo Films 201
Classic Sketches 209
The British Tours 217
The Final Curtain 221
The Laurel and Hardy Film Checklist 222
Sons of the Desert 225

Preface

Everybody can recall at least one sketch performed by Stan Laurel and Oliver Hardy, be it the famous pie fight, or their attempts to move a piano up a huge flight of steps. But how many can name the film their moment was from? This pocket reference book helps to answer these questions by identifying the films as well as the co-stars who appeared alongside them. Although this book concentrates specifically on the films of Laurel and Hardy, information regarding their early years, personal lives and later tours can be found in other publications, with the following titles particularly recommended;

MR. LAUREL AND MR. HARDY by John McCabe
ISBN 0-86051-327-0
LAUREL AND HARDY, THE MAGIC BEHIND THE MOVIES by Randy Skretvedt   ISBN 0-948820-65-9
BABE, THE LIFE OF OLIVER HARDY by John McCabe
ISBN 0 8605161 2 1
LAUREL AND HARDY, THE BRITISH TOURS by A. J. Marriot ISBN 0-9521308-0-7
THE COMEDY WORLD OF STAN LAUREL by John McCabe
ISBN 0-86051-635-0
LAUREL AND HARDY by McCabe, Bann and Kilgore
ISBN 0-76070-224-1
THE LAUREL AND HARDY ENCYCLOPEDIA by Glenn Mitchell ISBN 0 7134 7711 3
LAUREL OR HARDY by Rob Stone
ISBN 0 9652384 0 7
THE LAUREL & HARDY STOCK COMPANY by Leo M. Brooks ISBN 90 9010461 5
THE LAUREL AND HARDY DIGEST by Willie McIntyre
ISBN 0 9532958 0 X

It has taken over five years to collect all the available films on video and to put together a synopsis for each of the 106 films they performed together. With the help of other "Sons Of The Desert" (The Laurel and Hardy Appreciation Society), it has been possible to identify the majority of actors who appeared alongside them, and who undoubtedly contributed into making Stan and Ollie the greatest comedy team of all time.

INTRODUCTION

By the time Ollie (born Norvell Hardy, January 18, 1892) was born in the sleepy town of Harlem, Georgia, USA, his comic partner-to-be (born Arthur Stanley Jefferson, June 16, 1890) was already finding his feet playing in the back streets of Ulverston, a town in the north west of England.

Both youngsters were moulded by prominent parents. Ollie's father, a civil war veteran, died when Ollie was less than one year old, leaving his mother to bear the brunt of bringing up the boy along with his four step-brothers and sisters, while still becoming a successful hotel manageress. In England, young Stan's father was also an astute businessman, managing a string of theatres in Northern England and Scotland.

It was obvious from an early age that both boys loved to perform. Stan would watch and mimic the artists performing in his father's theatres, while Ollie would exercise his excellent singing voice at every given opportunity. Stan made his stage debut at the tender age of sixteen, before touring all over the country with a pantomime group, playing alongside the famous comedian of the time, Wee Georgie Wood. In 1910 Stan got his big break when he was offered a job by Fred Karno (Fred Wescott) of Fred Karno's London Comedians fame, who at the time was England's most successful showman. Among the comedians on the books was a young Londoner whom Stan admired greatly, and became understudy to. His name was Charlie Chaplin. At the same time Ollie, now living in Milledgeville, found work at the first movie house to open in town, where his chores included singing to the slides being shown.

The great divide of the Atlantic Ocean, which had so far kept the boys apart, diminished somewhat when Karno's troupe was invited to perform their highly acclaimed show *Mumming Birds* in America, under the title *A Night In An English Music Hall*. It was a smash hit, and they were invited back again in 1912. However, when the star of the show, Charlie Chaplin, quit to try his luck in movies the troupe, minus it's major asset, soon disbanded. They sailed back to England but Stan made the bold decision to stay in the States, trying to make a living in vaudeville, openly impersonating Chaplin. In 1913 Ollie caught the movie bug and moved to Jacksonville where he started working for the Lubin Film Company, making his debut appearance in a film called OUTWITTING DAD made in 1914. He earned himself a contract and was billed as "Babe Hardy," a nickname soon acquired after arriving at Lubin. Some 50 films later, and now employed at Vim, he played in a series of films called Plump and Runt.

Stan meanwhile, had struggled to earn a living on the stage but was approached in 1917, while appearing in Los Angeles, to make a film. His performance in NUTS IN MAY proved good enough to warrant Universal signing him up to play a character called Hickory Hiram in a series of one-reelers. A year later Stan signed up with Hal Roach, an up-and-coming movie producer. After a brief spell with Roach he starred in the two-reeler THE LUCKY DOG produced by "Broncho Billy" Anderson. The film made around 1920 would have been long forgotten today but for the fact that the "heavy" recruited to play the part of the robber was Oliver Norvell Hardy.

The rest, as they say is history, and in less than a decade Stan and Ollie became the most popular comedy duo ever. They portrayed "life's great losers," living in a world just beyond their comprehension. In real life, Stan was the exact opposite of his screen character. He was a perfectionist and the driving force behind the team, working tirelessly on the writing directing and editing aspects of production. All this with the blessing of Ollie, who was happy to leave it all in the more-than-capable hands of his comic partner and friend (many have commented that Stan was the uncredited director for the majority of the Hal Roach/Laurel and Hardy films, with the actual director in the chair merely a pawn manipulated by Stan).

Today their warmth, sincerity and universal appeal have failed to be bettered or matched, and their popularity still remains strong some eighty years on from their first screen escapade.

HAL ROACH

"To whom we are eternally grateful."

January 1892 became a significant period in the story of Laurel and Hardy. Not only did it signal the arrival of Oliver Hardy into the world, it also brought forth Stan and Ollie's future creator and mentor, Hal Roach. He was born of Irish descent in Elmira, New York, four days before Ollie on January 14, as Harry Eugene Roach (later to change his Christian name to Hal). He left home at seventeen to find work, and while employed in Los Angeles answered a newspaper advert to appear as an extra in a Western movie. His love affair with motion pictures had begun. While at Universal he became acquainted with fellow extra Harold Lloyd. In 1914 Roach took up producing and directing and recruited Lloyd to make a series of short films, which were bought by Pathé Exchange. By 1917 Roach and Lloyd had hit the big time, so in 1919 the young producer decided to build his own studios on a plot of land acquired in the Los Angeles district of Culver City. There Lloyd became a big star, as did others such as Snub Pollard, with Roach's Our Gang Series also proving to be a huge hit when first shown in 1922. Lloyd eventually left to form his own company while Roach continued to make worthwhile comedies, with his All Star Series this time very popular. Among the supporting actors were Stan Laurel and Oliver Hardy, who would soon graduate from playing small roles alongside regular performers such as James Finlayson and Charley Chase, to become the best loved clowns in movie history.

Hal Roach 1892-1992

A young Stan (standing) with Charlie Chaplin (seated right)
in the Fred Karno hockey team

Ethel Burton and Babe Hardy in THE SCHOLAR (1918)

An early shot of Stan

Stan (second left) with Charlie Chaplin (standing second right) and Karno manager Alf Reeves (standing far right)

Laurel and Hardy
SHORT FILM GUIDE

All Films Listed In Production Order.

(Film Abbreviations):
S   = Silent Short
SC* = Silent Cameo Appearance
T   = Talking Short
TC = Talking Cameo Appearance
F   = Feature
FC = Feature Cameo Appearance
4R = Four Reeler
DC = Documentary Cameo Appearance
Pg = Page Number

* As *Laurel and Hardy* only.

CAMERAS ROLL, ACTION!
THE SILENT FILMS

THE LUCKY DOG (S) Pg27 - Stan is thrown out of his lodgings and befriended by a stray dog. He then foils a robber (Ollie), and ruins a dog show, and later falls foul of Ollie and his associate.

45 MINUTES FROM HOLLYWOOD (S) Pg28 - A country boy goes to Hollywood and becomes innocently involved in a bank robbery. Ollie plays a detective while Stan is an out-of-work actor.

DUCK SOUP (S) Pg29 - Tramps Stan and Ollie take refuge in a vacated mansion posing as the owner and maid.

SLIPPING WIVES (S) Pg30 - Stan is hired to flirt with a lady to make her work occupied husband jealous. Ollie is her butler.

LOVE 'EM AND WEEP (S) Pg31 - James Finlayson is a rich businessman being blackmailed by an old flame. Stan plays his aide and Ollie a dinner guest.

WHY GIRLS LOVE SAILORS (S) Pg34 - Stan's girl is kidnapped by a rough sea captain, so he plans to steal her back by dressing as a man-eating blonde. Ollie is the second mate.

WITH LOVE AND HISSES (S) Pg35 - Stan is a recruit in the army, bullied by the sergeant (Ollie) and the captain (James Finlayson).

SAILORS, BEWARE! (S) Pg37 - Cab driver Stan foils the plans of two jewel thieves while out at sea. Ollie flirts with the lady passengers as the ship's purser.

NOW I'LL TELL ONE (S) Pg38 - Charley Chase and wife have marriage problems and end up in court. Stan is the lawyer, Ollie a policeman.

DO DETECTIVES THINK? (S) Pg39 - The boys are hired by a judge to protect him, after the murderer he convicted, escapes.

FLYING ELEPHANTS (S) Pg40 - The King of the cave people decrees that all males should marry, with the boys fighting over the hand of the same girl.

SUGAR DADDIES (S) Pg41 - After a wild night out, James Finlayson wakes up to find out he is married. Ollie, his butler and Stan his attorney, try to help him out of the predicament.

THE SECOND HUNDRED YEARS (S) Pg42 - Stan and Ollie are convicts who escape by posing as painters, daubing everything in sight.

CALL OF THE CUCKOOS (SC) Pg43 - Max Davidson is trying to sell his house without much success due to the antics of his next-door neighbours, a bunch of screwy trainee radio announcers.

HATS OFF (S) Pg44 - The boys are washing machine salesmen who try to sell their wares up a huge flight of steps.

PUTTING PANTS ON PHILIP(S) Pg45 - Ollie is more than a little embarrassed by the arrival of his kilt wearing nephew (Stan) from Scotland.

THE BATTLE OF THE CENTURY (S) Pg47 - Stan is a useless boxer, so his manager (Ollie) buys some insurance for him, then tries to arrange an accident to cash in. This results in the biggest pie fight in movie history.

LEAVE 'EM LAUGHING (S) Pg48 - Stan has toothache, so Ollie persuades him to pay a visit to the dentist. They inhale too much laughing gas and cause chaos when they drive into a traffic jam.

THE FINISHING TOUCH (S) Pg49 - The boys have the job of completing a half built house, which when finished is soon in a sorry state.

FROM SOUP TO NUTS (S) Pg50 - As inexperienced waiters, the boys ruin the Culpeppers posh dinner party.

YOU'RE DARN TOOTIN' (S) Pg51 - The boys are out-of-work musicians, who try to earn a crust by busking on the street.

THEIR PURPLE MOMENT (S) Pg53 - Stan and Ollie have planned a secret night out from their domineering wives, but hit trouble when they can't pay their bill.

SHOULD MARRIED MEN GO HOME? (S) Pg54 - Stan interrupts the Hardy's quiet day at home. The boys then head to the golf course, resulting in a mass mud fight.

EARLY TO BED (S) Pg55 - Ollie inherits a fortune and employs Stan as his butler, who is soon the butt of all his master's practical jokes.

TWO TARS (S) Pg62 - As sailors on shore leave, the boys team up with girlfriends, and run into a traffic jam that results in a car wrecking spree.

HABEAS CORPUS (S) Pg63 - A mad scientist hires the boys to steal him a corpse from the cemetery in the dead of night.

WE FAW DOWN (S) Pg64 - The boys cheat on their wives by pretending to go to the theatre, but on the way to their poker game, they become involved with two ladies, not knowing that the theatre has burnt down.

LIBERTY (S) Pg65 - Escaped convicts Stan and Ollie find themselves at the top of a partially built skyscraper.

WRONG AGAIN (S) Pg66 - Laurel and Hardy are stable hands, who mistakenly think a stolen painting called "Blue Boy" is one of the horses they are looking after.

THAT'S MY WIFE (S) Pg67 - Ollie's uncle arrives in town promising his nephew a large inheritance as long as he is still happily married. As she has left home, Stan has to masquerade as Ollie's wife.

BIG BUSINESS (S) Pg68 - Trying to sell Christmas trees door-to-door sees the boys clash with James Finlayson. His house and their car bear the full brunt of the hostilities.

DOUBLE WHOOPEE (S) Pg70 - As doorman and footman at a swanky hotel, the boys soon upset a visiting Prince.

BACON GRABBERS (S) Pg71 - The boys are given the job of retrieving a radio from Edgar Kennedy.

ANGORA LOVE (S) Pg74 - A friendly goat attaches itself to Stan and Ollie. When they hear the goat has been stolen, they try to smuggle it past their strict landlord.

ANY NUTS? – THE "TALKIES"

UNACCUSTOMED AS WE ARE (T) Pg79 -Ollie brings Stan home for dinner, but when his wife leaves, Ollie tries to cook the meal himself.

BERTH MARKS (T) Pg80 -The boys are musicians on an overnight train bound for an engagement and cause a clothes ripping epidemic to break out.

MEN O' WAR (T) Pg81 - Stan and Ollie are sailors on leave, who team up with two ladies in the park, then create havoc on the boating lake.

THE HOLLYWOOD REVUE OF 1929 (TC) Pg82 - The boys play a small sketch in this star-studded Hollywood bash as bungling magicians.

PERFECT DAY (T) Pg83 - A picnic in the country is planned, but the boys, their wives and gout-ridden uncle never leave the street due to car problems and a war with the neighbours.

THEY GO BOOM (T) Pg84 - Ollie is poorly in bed, with Stan acting as his less-than-able nurse. A clash with the landlord sees their bed sit wrecked.

THE HOOSE-GOW (T) Pg85 - Members of a prison road gang, the boys clash with prison staff and visiting dignitaries and involve all in a mass rice fight.

THE ROGUE SONG (FC) Pg87 - Stan and Ollie appear in several sketches in this musical as sidekicks to a Russian bandit (Lawrence Tibbett) who has fallen for the princess of his deadly Cossack rivals.

NIGHT OWLS (T) Pg88 - The boys are caught sleeping on a park bench, so have to help Officer Kennedy redeem himself with the police chief, by robbing the chief's house.

BLOTTO (T) Pg89 - The boys visit a newly opened nightclub and get hopelessly "drunk" on liquor sabotaged by Stan's wife.

BRATS (T) Pg90 - Stan and Ollie have the dubious task of looking after their young sons.

BELOW ZERO (T) Pg92 - As street musicians in the middle of winter, the boys find a wallet in the snow; so take a policeman, who has saved them from a mugging, for a slap up meal.

HOG WILD (T) Pg93 - Ollie has the simple task of erecting a radio aerial on the roof. Stan arrives on the scene to lend a hand.

THE LAUREL - HARDY MURDER CASE (T) Pg94 - Ebeneezer Laurel has died, so the boys go to the reading of the will, spending the night in a large spooky house.

PARDON US (F) Pg95 - The boys are sent to prison for selling beer during prohibition. They escape and pose as cotton pickers to avoid recapture.

ANOTHER FINE MESS (T) Pg98 - Tramps Stan and Ollie take refuge from the law in a recently vacated mansion. When a Lord and Lady call, Ollie poses as the master of the house, with Stan as his butler and maid.

BE BIG (T) Pg99 - The Laurels and Hardys are off on vacation, until Stan and Ollie hear of a stag party being held by the gang in their honour.

CHICKENS COME HOME (T) Pg102 - Successful fertilizer dealer Ollie is running for mayor, until trouble looms when an old flame threatens blackmail.

THE STOLEN JOOLS (TC) Pg104 - Stan and Ollie are assistants to a detective in this all-star fund raising film.

LAUGHING GRAVY (T) Pg105 - The boys try to hide their pet dog from their strict landlord which results in them stranded on the snow covered roof.

OUR WIFE (T) Pg106 - Ollie has been forbidden to marry his sweetheart, so with Stan's help plans an elopement.

COME CLEAN (T) Pg107 - Stan and Ollie rescue a lady attempting suicide, then have the unenviable job of keeping her from their wives.

ONE GOOD TURN (T) Pg108 - As victims of the depression, the boys are forced to beg for a meal. When they overhear some amateur dramatics they think an old lady has been robbed so decide to help out.

BEAU HUNKS (4R) Pg110 - The boys join the Foreign Legion to help Ollie forget a broken romance. Unfortunately the other legionnaires are all heartbroken over the same girl.

ON THE LOOSE (TC) Pg111 - Two girlfriends are fed up with their dates for always taking them to Coney Island. Stan and Ollie call asking if the girls would go out on a trip...to Coney Island!

HELPMATES (T) Pg112 - Ollie throws a wild party while his wife is away. She decides to return home early, so Stan is recruited to help clean up.

ANY OLD PORT (T) Pg113 - Sailors Stan and Ollie prevent a tough hotel owner from forcing his cleaning girl into marriage. Stan then ends up in the boxing ring with him.

THE MUSIC BOX (T) Pg114 - The boys are deliverymen, given the job of delivering a piano up a huge flight of steps.

THE CHIMP (T) Pg116 - The circus goes bust, so all employees are given part of the show as severance pay. Stan gets the flea circus, Ollie, Ethel "The Human Chimpanzee."

COUNTY HOSPITAL (T) Pg118 - Ollie is recuperating in hospital, but the stay is short-lived when Stan pays a visit.

PACK UP YOUR TROUBLES (F) Pg119 - After the war, the boys go in search of their dead friend's baby girl, and then try to locate her grandparents, the "Smiths."

SCRAM! (T) Pg121 - The boys are told to leave town by an ill-tempered judge, who later finds them in his house and responsible for his wife's drunken state.

THEIR FIRST MISTAKE (T) Pg127 - Ollie is in trouble with his wife for always going out with Stan. Ollie then adopts a baby to solve his problems only to find his wife has left home.

TOWED IN A HOLE (T) Pg128 - The boys are fish sellers, who try to improve business by buying a boat.

TWICE TWO (T) Pg129 - Stan and Ollie have married each other's sisters. They celebrate their joint wedding anniversaries, which strains family loyalties.

FRA DIAVOLO (THE DEVIL'S BROTHER) (F) Pg129 - Robbed of their life savings in 18th Century Italy, Stanlio and Ollio decide to become bandits themselves - that is until they try to hold-up the notorious bandit Fra Diavolo.

ME AND MY PAL (T) Pg132 - Ollie's marriage to a rich oil tycoon's daughter is held up when the jigsaw Stan bought as a wedding present is found to have a piece missing.

THE MIDNIGHT PATROL (T) Pg133 - Police Officers Laurel and Hardy investigate a house break-in. The suspected culprit is apprehended but turns out to be the police chief himself.

BUSY BODIES (T) Pg133 - Working at the sawmill sees the boys clash with a fellow worker and wreck the foreman's hut and their car.

WILD POSES (TC) Pg134 - Spanky McFarland and family spend a day at the photographers, in this Our Gang short. The boys are briefly seen posing as babies.

DIRTY WORK (T) Pg135 - The boys are chimney sweeps who call on a mad scientist, who has just perfected his rejuvenation formula.

SONS OF THE DESERT (F) Pg136 - Sworn to attend a convention, Ollie feign illness to fool his wife, and along with Stan, pretends to go on a voyage to Honolulu.

HOLLYWOOD PARTY (FC) Pg138 - Schnarzan the jungle film star holds a party, which is gatecrashed by Stan and Ollie.

OLIVER THE EIGHTH (T) Pg139 - Ollie is accepted to be the new husband for a rich widow after she advertises in the newspaper. Unfortunately she has murderous tendencies towards anyone called Oliver.

GOING BYE-BYE! (T) Pg141 - As key witnesses at a murder trial, the boys are advised to leave town. The killer then escapes seeking revenge.

THEM THAR HILLS (T) Pg141 - Ollie has gout, so is prescribed a trip into the mountains by his doctor. With Stan in tow and after drinking plenty of the mountain "water" a feud soon develops with a fellow traveller.

BABES IN TOYLAND (F) Pg143 - Ollie Dee and Stannie Dum try to prevent the marriage of Toyland's meanest resident Silas Barnaby to Little Bo Peep.

THE LIVE GHOST (T) Pg148 - The boys help the captain of a so-called "ghost ship" shanghai a crew, but end up aboard themselves when the ship sets sail.

TIT FOR TAT (T) Pg151 - Stan and Ollie open up an electrical store next door to a grocer, who accuses Ollie of chasing after his wife.

THE FIXER-UPPERS (T) Pg152 - As greeting card salesmen, Stan and Ollie agree to help a lady with her marital problems.

BONNIE SCOTLAND (F) Pg153 - Stan and Ollie escape from prison to Scotland for the reading of Stan's late grandfather's will, and inadvertently join the army.

THICKER THAN WATER (T) Pg155 - Stan persuades Ollie to draw out the Hardy savings to pay off a furniture bill, only to blow it all on a grandfather clock.

THE BOHEMIAN GIRL (F) Pg156 - As gypsies, the boys are left to bring up a kidnapped child, taken from her father, by the vengeful lover of Ollie's wife.

OUR RELATIONS (F) Pg161 - Stan and Ollie's nautical twin brothers hit town on shore leave to deliver a valuable ring. Mistaken identities cause major trouble for both sets of twins.

ON THE WRONG TREK (TC) Pg163 - Charley Chase and family are robbed as they drive to their vacation. The boys appear very briefly as hitchhikers.

WAY OUT WEST (F) Pg165 - The boys travel to Brushwood Gulch to deliver a deed to a gold mine, but are duped into handing it over to the saloon owners.

PICK A STAR (FC) Pg167 - A small time singer wins a talent contest and ends up fulfilling her dreams in Hollywood. Stan and Ollie play two small sketches.

SWISS MISS (F) Pg169 - Stan and Ollie are in Switzerland trying to sell mousetraps. When they can't pay for a meal they are put to work in the hotel.

BLOCK-HEADS (F) Pg170 - In the army again during World War One, Stan is left to guard the post, which he does long after the war's end. Ollie sets out to find his old buddy and bring him home for a slap-up meal.

A CHUMP AT OXFORD (F) Pg172 - Street cleaners Stan and Ollie foil a bank raid and are rewarded with scholarships to Oxford University. There Stan, due to an accident, becomes Lord Paddington, Oxford's greatest ever athlete and scholar.

THE FLYING DEUCES (F) Pg174 - While holidaying in Paris, Ollie falls hopelessly in love with the innkeeper's daughter. When his advances are rejected, the boys join the Foreign Legion.

SAPS AT SEA (F) Pg176 - Ollie has a nervous breakdown while working in a horn factory and is prescribed an ocean voyage by his doctor. The boys find themselves adrift at sea with an escaped convict for company.

THEIR FINAL REEL

GREAT GUNS (F) Pg183 - The boys join the army to look after their rich master, and try to fend off a local girl who they think is a "gold-digger."

A-HAUNTING WE WILL GO (F) Pg184 - The police are after a crook, who hides in a coffin, escorted by Stan and Ollie, so he can claim a scam inheritance.

AIR RAID WARDENS (F) Pg185 - The boys run a cycle shop during the Second World War, and try to do their bit by joining the Civil Defence.

JITTERBUGS (F) Pg187 - As travelling musicians, the boys help a girl's mother who has been swindled.

THE TREE IN A TEST TUBE (DC) Pg189 - Stan and Ollie star in a colour documentary about the importance of wood in the war effort.

THE DANCING MASTERS (F) Pg190 - The dancing school run by Stan and Ollie faces closure, as the boys help demonstrate a revolutionary ray gun.

THE BIG NOISE (F) Pg191 - An inventor hires the boys to guard his super bomb. They have to fight off a gang of crooks intent on selling it to the enemy.

NOTHING BUT TROUBLE (F) Pg192 - The boys are servants hired to work at a royal dinner party. They become friends with the young King, who is in grave danger from his scheming uncle.

THE BULLFIGHTERS (F) Pg194 - Private detectives Laurel and Hardy are on the trail of Larceny Nell in Mexico. There Stan is mistaken for a world famous bullfighter.

ATOLL K (F) Pg197 - Stan inherits a yacht and a South Sea island, but a storm beaches them on a uranium-laden atoll. Treasure seekers flood the atoll which duly sinks.

The ratings in the main part of the book have been calculated from a poll of 100 prominent members from the European "Sons of the Desert," the official Laurel and Hardy Appreciation Society.

The Ratings are as follows:

N/A	Very little L&H content or film not available for showing
5	Poor
5+	Poor to Average
6	Average
6+	Average to Quite Good
7	Quite Good
7+	Quite Good to Good
8	Good
8+	Good to Very Good
9	Very Good
9+	Very Good to Excellent
10	Excellent

Footers in the book are Classic Lines, Title Cards and Did You Knows?

Cameras Roll, Action!
The Silent Films

Cameras Roll, Action!

THE LUCKY DOG 5+

Directed by **Jess Robbins**, Produced by **Gilbert M. Anderson**, Filmed - circa 1920, Released - 1922 by Metro, Running time - 2 reels.

With: **Stan Laurel** (Man with stray dog), **Oliver Hardy** (The robber), **Florence Gillet** (Stan's lady friend).

Stan is thrown onto the street for not paying his rent, where a small dog befriends him. Walking down the street, he stumbles upon a hold-up, just as the robber (Ollie) is relieving his victim of his money, which he then unwittingly places in Stan's back pocket. Ollie attempts to rob Stan as well, but he manages to escape. The small dog makes friends with a poodle, whose lady owner persuades Stan to enter his dog in the local dog show. The entry is refused nevertheless as the show is for thoroughbreds only. Stan sneaks in on all fours only to be slung out, closely followed by all the dogs in the show that run out into the street. Stan spots his lady friend searching for her dog and offers his own as consolation. She accepts his gesture and offers him a lift to her home, leaving her boyfriend behind feeling angry and jealous. He bumps into the robber, and between them they plan their revenge on Stan. At the lady's house, Stan is joined by the boyfriend and Ollie who is introduced as the "Count de Chease of Switzerland." Ollie tries to shoot Stan but his gun jams, so attempts to blow him up with a stick of dynamite, as the spurned boyfriend chases the lady around the house after having his marriage proposal refused. Fortunately for Stan and his girl, the dog picks up the dynamite and chases their attackers into the garden where they are blown up as they hide behind a bush.

'Put 'em up insect, before I comb your hair with lead.' Ollie's order to Stan, was their first on-screen communication, conveyed with the help of a title card. A long-standing debate continues regarding the actual date THE LUCKY DOG was filmed. Evidence suggests it took place sometime between September 1920 and January 1921, and not 1919 as first suggested (In a 1957 interview Stan thought the film was made around 1916-17). Stan and Ollie's paths would cross several times before they appeared in their next film together. Stan returned to vaudeville treading the boards until 1922 when Gilbert Anderson found backing for a series of Laurel comedies. The Laurel/Anderson films released by Metro included a clever parody of the Rudolph Valentino smash BLOOD AND SAND, re-

(Stan) 'No use crying over split milk.' *(THE FLYING DEUCES)*

What Was The Film When..?

titled MUD AND SAND, with Stan playing the lead as Rhubarb Vaselino. Ollie continued to work in pictures, mainly for Vitagraph, regularly turning out a film every month. Stan joined the Hal Roach camp for the second time (he had worked for Roach at Rolin in 1918 where he had made five one-reelers, with three directed by Roach himself) in March 1923, continuing to make parodies of well-known films, before Roach terminated his contract. Joe Rock signed him up in 1924, but he returned to the Roach Studios in May 1925 as a writer and director, having an agreement with Rock not to appear in front of the camera while Rock was promoting his Laurel films. Stan directed the James Finlayson short YES YES NANETTE, with Oliver Hardy also in the cast. Ollie had signed a long term contract with Roach in February 1926 and was due to play the role of the butler in the Harry Myers film GET 'EM YOUNG. Fate played a part when Ollie was scalded during a cooking accident at home and Stan, the original director of the film, was asked to stand in. Reluctantly Stan agreed, despite his agreement with Joe Rock and his preference for writing and directing. In this film (now directed by Fred Guiol), Stan would include a whimpering cry that was to become one of his legendary trademarks. Just one month after completion, Stan and Ollie would appear in their second film together, 45 MINUTES FROM HOLLYWOOD, the first of many under the guiding hand of Hal Roach.

45 MINUTES FROM HOLLYWOOD

Directed by **Fred Guiol**, Produced by **Hal Roach**, Filmed - August 1926, Released - December 26 1926 by Pathé, Running time - 2 reels.

With: **Glenn Tryon** (Country boy, Orville), **Rube Clifford** (Father), **Charlotte Mineau** (Mother), **Sue O'Neil** (Sister), **Oliver Hardy** (House detective), **Stan Laurel** (Out-of-work actor), **Edna Murphy** (Ollie's jealous wife), **Tiny Sandford** (Conductor).

Also appeared: Theda Bara, Jerry Mandy, Ham Kinsey, Ed Brandenberg, Jack Hill, Al Hallet, Our Gang Kids, Hal Roach Bathing Beauties.

The bright lights of Hollywood beckon for Orville, a country boy who has a family debt to pay off. Whilst out sightseeing, he encounters a gang of robbers pulling off a job while masquerading as a film crew. They escape in their getaway car but the "lady" member of the gang falls out into the boy's arms. The police

(Title card) Gabriel honk your horn! (*LOVE 'EM AND WEEP*)

Cameras Roll, Action!

pursue the pair down the street where they take refuge in a hotel room while the occupant (Ollie) takes a bath. The "lady" robber turns out to be in drag and knocks out Orville before swapping clothes and stealing his money. Ollie discovers him, now attired in a dress and laying unconscious on the bed, just as his wife returns. She throws Orville out of the window before turning angrily on her husband. The boy meanwhile is chased by the police, believing him to be the lady robber. He re-enters the hotel and puts on a pair of Ollie's trousers before bumping into his assailant, with the ensuing fight spilling into another room where a guest (Stan) also becomes caught up in the struggle. During the punch up the boy retrieves his money, and when Ollie and the police arrive on the scene the real crook is arrested. Ollie however, is not in a forgiving mood and chases Orville down the stairs clutching a fire extinguisher. He throws the extinguisher which lodges down the back of the boy's oversized trousers, spraying the on-looking hotel guests.

45 MINUTES FROM HOLLYWOOD, the first Hal Roach film in which Stan and Ollie both appeared, was notable for the fact that they did not have a single scene together. Making his debut in this film was Stanley (Tiny) Sandford (born Iowa, 1894), who would make 23 appearances with Stan and Ollie in a ten-year spell, as well as appearing in several Chaplin films. Jack Hill also made the first of 34 appearances with the boys, employed mainly as an extra and bit part actor.

DUCK SOUP

Directed by **Fred Guiol**, Produced by **Hal Roach**, Filmed - Sep 1926, Released - Mar 13, 1927 by Pathé, Running time - 2 reels.

With: **Stan Laurel** (James Hives), **Oliver Hardy** (Marmaduke Maltravers), **Madeline Hurlock** (Lady Tarbotham), **William Austin** (Lord Tarbotham), **Bob Kortman** (Ranger rounding up vagrants).

Down-and-outs Stan and Ollie are reading newspapers in the park, when Ollie spots the headlines about forest rangers enlisting vagrants to fight forest fires. Stan notices the conscription taking place, with the rangers bullying the park layabouts into signing up. When they too are approached, the boys run off, making their getaway on a stolen bicycle. They find themselves in the gardens of a large mansion and enter the house by way of the open

(Student) 'Oh pardon me, but haven't you come to the wrong college?' (Ollie) 'Well this is Oxford isn't it?' (Student) 'Yes, but your dressed for Eton.' (Stan) 'Well that's swell, we haven't eaten since breakfast.' (*A CHUMP AT OXFORD*)

French windows, just as the servants are leaving. Stan checks the front door and finds a note declaring that the owner, Colonel Blood, is away on vacation and the house is available for rent. They prepare themselves a slap-up meal and are just settling down in their lavish surroundings when the front door bell rings, the callers being a Lord and Lady keen to rent. Ollie quickly devises a plan for himself to play the role of the colonel and Stan the maid. Stan, attired in the maid's uniform and a wig, lets the couple in. Ollie interrupts his piano playing to try and locate the billiard room for the inquisitive Lord, while Stan is quizzed by his wife about the house. Happy with the mansion, the couple decide to accept the offer. The boys are about to leave, when the real proprietor of the house returns having cut short his trip after forgetting his bow and arrow, which Ollie is in the process of breaking in half to put into a packing case. Stan recognises the colonel from a portrait hanging on the wall and pushes him into the closet, but he escapes, and when confronted by the Lord, chases him around the house with all guns blazing. A removal van arrives, but when Stan goes outside to help load the cases, a ranger is waiting and his cover is blown. The rangers storm the house and capture Stan and Ollie, before taking them away to work on the forest blaze.

Based on *Home From The Honeymoon* written in 1908 by Stan's father, Arthur Jefferson. Although the potential for a team was still to be realised, DUCK SOUP was regarded by many as the first "true" Laurel and Hardy film. Future mannerisms and trademarks first surfaced in this film, including Ollie's domineering disposition over his less-than-confident partner. DUCK SOUP was considered a lost film, until its discovery in the early 1970's.

SLIPPING WIVES

Directed by **Fred Guiol**, Produced by **Hal Roach**, Edited by **Richard Currier**, Filmed - Oct 1926, Released - Apr 3, 1927 by Pathé, Running time - 2 reels.

With: **Stan Laurel** (Ferdinand Flamingo), **Oliver Hardy** (Jarvis the butler), **Priscilla Dean** (Wife), **Herbert Rawlinson** (Artist husband, Leon), **Albert Conti** (Wife's friend, Hon. Winchester Squirtz).

"The story of a drifting husband and wife who no longer talked to each other - They barked."

Cameras Roll, Action!

An artist is so occupied with his work that he completely ignores the affections of his wife. One of the lady's friend's hits upon the idea of her flirting openly with a stranger in a bid to make her husband jealous and re-ignite the spark currently missing from their relationship. Delivery boy, Ferdinand Flamingo (Stan), arrives at the front door with supplies and earns the instant dislike of the butler (Ollie) when he refuses to go to the service entrance. A struggle breaks out resulting in Ollie covered in paint. After a little persuasion, Stan agrees to be the lady's "lover" for the day and is taken upstairs by the butler to get washed and changed, where Ollie gets his own back by roughly giving him a bath fully clothed. Stan makes his way downstairs where he is introduced as a famous writer and puts on a one man show of "Samson and Delilah," his latest venture. Stan mistakes the lady's friend for her husband, and with the plan obviously not working, is taken for a drink, returning to the lounge much the worse for wear. He continues to flirt in front of the wrong man, not knowing that husband and wife have in the meantime settled their differences. A chase develops through the house with Ollie, armed with a shotgun, running Stan through the front door. However, Ollie shoots a policeman in the backside by mistake and returns to the house sporting a black eye.

Apart from two scenes together, Stan and Ollie were again cast in direct opposition. Although memorable for Stan's one-man parody of "Samson and Delilah," the chemistry produced between the boys in their previous film was sadly lacking in this one. Ollie would appear in two more Roach shorts before playing alongside Stan in LOVE 'EM AND WEEP.

LOVE 'EM AND WEEP

Directed by **Fred Guiol**, Produced by **Hal Roach**, Filmed - Jan 1927, Released - Jun 12, 1927 by Pathé, Running time - 2 reels.

With: **James Finlayson** (Titus Tillsbury), **Stan Laurel** (Romaine Ricketts), **Mae Busch** (Blackmailer), **Charlotte Mineau** (Mrs Aggie Tillsbury), **Charlie Hall** (Butler), **Vivien Oakland** (Mrs Ricketts), **Oliver Hardy** (Judge Chigger), **Gale Henry ?** ("Town snoop"), **May Wallace** (Mrs Chigger), **Ed Brandenberg** (Waiter).

Ancient Proverb: "Every married man should have his fling - but be careful not to get flung too far."

What Was The Film When..?

Titus Tillsbury, a rich and successful businessman, is rehearsing a speech in front of his aide Romaine Ricketts (Stan), when an old girlfriend bursts into the office. All becomes clear when she produces an old photograph of her and Titus together in their bathing costumes. When she tells him that the newspapers might be interested in the photo, Titus succumbs to the blackmail threat and agrees to meet her later that evening to discuss the matter. Stan informs him that his wife is in the building, so the blackmailer is bundled into the bathroom just as Mrs Tillsbury enters the office. She reminds her husband of the dinner party they are hosting later that evening to which she has invited Judge Chigger (Ollie) and his wife among the influential guests. Stan is asked to help his boss out of the tricky situation by taking the blackmailer to the Pink Pup club and stalling her until he arrives. At first Stan refuses, fearful of being caught out by his own jealous wife, but soon changes his mind when given the alternative - the sack! Later that evening Stan arrives to pick up his "date" who is less than pleased with Stan's explanation that his boss will join them after singing his wife to sleep. At the dinner party the guests demand a song from their host who is handed the words to *You May Be Fast, But Your Momma's Gonna Slow You Down*. Back at the club, the blackmailer has had enough of waiting about and storms outside, where Stan is wrestled to the ground for the car keys, all witnessed by the "town snoop" who heads off to inform Stan's wife of the goings-on. Stan and the blackmailer arrive at the dinner party with Titus singing an even more appropriate song *Somebody's Coming To My House*. Titus introduces them as Mr. and Mrs Ricketts before confronting his old girlfriend and telling her he will shoot himself, at which point she duly faints. He explains to his wife that his guest has fainted from sunstroke, so Mrs Tillsbury insists that Stan and his "wife" stay the night and goes off to prepare a room. They decide to sneak the unconscious lady out by sitting her on Titus's back and then draping a long coat over them to complete the disguise. Stan escorts his "wife" out of the door but Mrs Tillsbury isn't fooled by the strange sight and follows them out armed with a walking stick. Stan gets to the bottom of the path only to be confronted by the real Mrs Ricketts, and the two aggrieved wives set about their husbands as the blackmailer recovers and runs away.

LOVE 'EM AND WEEP marked the acting debuts alongside the boys of Mae Busch (born South Melbourne, Australia, June 18, 1891), James Finlayson and Charlie Hall, who between them would make over 90 appearances in Laurel and Hardy films. James Henderson Finlayson (born Larbert, Scotland, August 27, 1887) would become the boys' main adversary during their thirteen-year

(Title card) If you must make a noise – make it quietly (*THE FINISHING TOUCH*)

Cameras Roll, Action!

Charlie Hall
1899 - 1959

screen relationship, appearing in 33 Laurel and Hardy films. "Fin" learned his trade with Mack Sennett before joining up with Hal Roach in 1923, where his unmistakable squint and false bushy moustache became his famous trademarks. He was best remembered for his many run-ins with the boys, including the irate customer in BIG BUSINESS (1929), Lord Rocburg in FRA DIAVOLO (1933) and as Mickey Finn in WAY OUT WEST (1937).

WHY GIRLS LOVE SAILORS

Directed by **Fred Guiol**, Produced by **Hal Roach**, Filmed - Feb 1927, Released - Jul 17, 1927 by Pathé, Running time - 2 reels.

With: **Stan Laurel** (Willie Brisling), **Viola Richard** (Willie's fiancée, Nelly), **Malcolm Waite** (Captain), **Oliver Hardy** (Second mate), **Anita Garvin** (Captain's wife).

Also appeared: Bobby Dunn?

St. Amieux, a delightful little fishing port where the crew of *The Belle Morue* are loading cargo. Nearby, sweethearts Willie Brisling (Stan) and his fiancée Nelly are engrossed in their love for each other, that is until the tough sea captain of *The Belle Morue* takes a shine to Nelly and drags her off to his ship. Despite Stan's attempts to stop him, he proves no match and is tossed like a rag doll into the fishing nets. Stan climbs aboard the boat and scares a crew member by tucking his head under his jumper, pretending to be a headless ghost. Hiding inside a trunk of theatre props, Stan hits upon the idea of dressing up as a floozy to woo the captain and rescue his loved one. In a flowing dress and a blonde wig, he soon has the crew swooning, especially when the wind blows up his dress to reveal frilly bloomers! After openly flirting with the crew and the second mate (Ollie), Stan turns his attention to the captain and is sitting on his knee when the captain's wife returns to the boat having a month's worth of marital arguments to catch up on. She pulls a shotgun on her cheating husband and is about to pull the trigger when Stan whips off his wig to reveal his true identity. The captain pretends that it's all been a test to see if his wife really loves him. The couple embrace but the moment is spoilt as Stan introduces Nelly and tells the captain's wife that the four other girls have already left. Once again the captain is in the doghouse as Stan and his girl escape.

(Conductor) 'What are you fellows going to do in Pottsville?' (Ollie) 'We're a big time vaudeville act.' (Conductor) 'Well I'll bet you're good.' (*BERTHMARKS*)

Cameras Roll, Action!

WHY GIRLS LOVE SAILORS, like DUCK SOUP, was considered a lost film until it apparently turned up playing in Paris in 1971 (a private collector confirmed the film's existance in 1985). The discovery put many wrongs to right, including Ollie's role in the film which was originally listed as that of the captain. It also marked the first of Anita Garvin's (born New York, February 11, 1907?) 11 appearances with the boys. Her debut had primarily been listed as being in WITH LOVE AND HISSES, their next film.

WITH LOVE AND HISSES

Directed by **Fred Guiol**, Produced by **Hal Roach**, Filmed - Mar 1927, Released - Aug 28, 1927 by Pathé, Running time - 2 reels.

With: **Stan Laurel** (Cuthbert Hope), **Oliver Hardy** (Top Sergeant Banner), **James Finlayson** (Captain Bustle), **Frank Brownlee** (Major General Rohrer), **Eve Southern**, **Anita Garvin** (Captain's lady friends), **Jerry Mandy** (Hungry soldier on train), **Will Stanton** (Soldier asleep by Stan).

Also appeared: Chet Brandenberg, Frank Saputo, Josephine Dunn.

"There were cheers and kisses as the Home Guards left for camp - the married men did the cheering."

Private Cuthbert Hope (Stan) arrives at the railway station where the troops are about to embark for camp. On the train he soon upsets his superiors when he settles down in the captain's private berth. A sergeant (Ollie) claims the berth for himself, before being reprimanded by the captain and ordered to report next morning. Stan finds himself a seat cramped together with other soldiers, sitting opposite one with a ravenous appetite. Stan is offered a pie but throws it out of the window, splatting the captain full in the face as he takes in some fresh air from his berth directly behind them. At Camp Klaxon the recruits are taken on a long march. Three hours later and still two miles from camp, the troops notice a creek and decide to cool off with a spot of "skinny dipping." Stan is ordered to guard the clothes but the temptation for him is too great and he jumps in as well, unaware that Ollie's discarded cigarette has set the pile of uniforms ablaze. Back at camp the major general arrives to inspect the men, so when the bathers hear the bugle call they go to dress, only to find their clothes in a smouldering heap. The naked men

(Title card) He left his watch to square the thirty cents – It was that kind of a watch
(*SHOULD MARRIED MEN GO HOME?*)

James Finlayson and friend larking around on the Roach lot

Cameras Roll, Action!

hide behind a billboard advertising a Cecil B. DeMille production *The Volga Boatmen*. They pull up the billboard and stick their heads through, replacing those of the boatmen on the poster. A skunk forces the men to beat a hasty retreat, and in their rush to get away, they upset a beehive. The swarm follows them back to camp causing mayhem amongst the troops and visiting dignitaries.

Ollie, who had only played bit parts in the previous three films, co-starred in their first army venture as the brash Top Sergeant Banner, with Stan the main target for his bullying. Confrontations with James Finlayson would prove a prosperous formula for hilarity throughout the Roach period of Stan and Ollie's film careers.

SAILORS, BEWARE!

Directed by **Hal Yates**, Produced by **Hal Roach**, Filmed - Apr 1927, Released - Sep 25, 1927 by Pathé, Running time - 2 reels.

With: **Stan Laurel** (Chester Chaste), **Oliver Hardy** (Purser Cryder), **Anita Garvin** (Madame Ritz), **Harry Earles** (Midget husband, Roger), **Frank Brownlee** (Captain Bull), **Lupe Velez** (Baroness Behr), **Will Stanton** (Baron Behr), **Tiny Sandford** (Passenger on steamship).

Also appeared: Viola Richard, May Wallace, Connie Evans, Barbara Pierce, Ed Brandenberg, Dorothy Coburn, Charley Young.

Cab driver Chester Chaste (Stan) is taking Madame Ritz and her midget husband (disguised as a baby) to the docks, where the pair board the *S S Mirimar*, Monte Carlo bound for the races. Unknown to Stan, his passengers are international crook's intent on robbing the ship's wealthy passengers. On the quayside Stan is distracted by a fire that breaks out in the back of his cab and before he realises it, his cab is hauled aboard and the ship has set sail. Stan reports the incident to the purser (Ollie) who, pre-occupied with the lady passengers, sends him to see Captain Bull, reputed to be the toughest skipper on the seven seas. The captain brands him a stowaway and puts him to work as a steward. While Madame Ritz plans the robbery by organising a bridge game, Stan calls at her cabin with drinks and becomes involved in a rigged dice game with her husband that soon renders him penniless. Later at the bridge game, the midget climbs from his pram and relieves the unsuspecting players of their jewellery, stuffing it inside his toy doll. On the way back to his cabin, he bumps into Stan who demands his money back from the dice game. The midget refuses the request so Stan throws the doll down a ventilation shaft. The thief dives headfirst after it, landing in a pile of soot at the bottom. The captain orders Stan to give the supposed infant a bath, but when they reach the bathroom, he encounters fierce resistance from the midget who is reluctant to be undressed. Stan finally manages the task and notices "the baby" has a hairy chest. With the midget's cover blown, Stan finds the doll stuffed with jewellery and marches into the recreation room to inform everyone that the thief has been apprehended. A collection is taken up for the hero as Madame Ritz is also arrested. Stan takes his opportunity to repay Ollie for all the bullying he has endured by delivering him a swift kick up the backside. Thinking it was the midget who delivered the blow, Ollie squares up to the mini-villain, but turns out to be no match and ends up in a battered heap on the stairs.

The evolution of Stan and Ollie's characters was nowhere near completion, especially in this film. Stan's was brash and confident, only occasionally drifting into the dimwit role he would make so famous.

NOW I'LL TELL ONE

Directed by **James Parrott**, Produced by **Hal Roach**, Released - Oct 9, 1927 by Pathé, Running time - 2 reels.

With: **Charley Chase** (Husband), **Edna Marian** (Wife), **Stan Laurel** (Lawyer), **Oliver Hardy** (Policeman), **Will R. Walling** (Judge).

Also appeared: Lincoln Plumer.

Charley and his wife have a bust-up and end up in the divorce court. His wife spins a fantastic yarn about all the abuse she has suffered at the hands of her husband. Charley's lawyer (Stan) is as dumb as they come and of very little help. The trial becomes unruly, and as the courtroom collapses all around them, the warring couple decide to make up.

Very little was initially known about this "lost" Charley Chase short. It had been originally listed as a Stan Laurel solo performance, until the second reel of the film was recently discovered in 1989, showing Ollie, appearing briefly as a cop. Storyline and production dates are vague (it was released after SAILORS, BEWARE!) but it is now officially listed as a film in which both the boys performed, with the new total amended to 106.

(Stan) 'Well Oliver, I hope you grow up to be as good a mother as your father.' (THE BOHEMIAN GIRL)

Cameras Roll, Action!

DO DETECTIVES THINK?

Directed by **Fred Guiol**, Produced by **Hal Roach**, Filmed - May 1927, Released - Nov 20, 1927 by Pathé, Running time - 2 reels.

With: **Stan Laurel** (Ferdinand Finkleberry), **Oliver Hardy** (Sherlock Pinkham), **James Finlayson** (Judge Foozle), **Noah Young** (The Tipton Slasher), **Frank Brownlee** (Detective Agency boss), **Viola Richard** (Mrs Foozle), **Will Stanton** (Slasher's side-kick), **Charles Bachman** (Policeman).

"This story opens with a lot of people in court - most of them should be in jail."

The jury at a murder trial finds the accused "The Tipton Slasher" guilty, so Judge Foozle sentences him to be hanged, with the murderer vowing to escape and take his revenge. One morning the judge nearly chokes on his breakfast when he reads the headlines in the newspaper - THROAT SLASHER IN SENSATIONAL ESCAPE - so he rings a detective agency asking to hire the bravest men on the books. The job is given to Ferdinand Finkleberry (Stan) and Sherlock Pinkham (Ollie), who just happen to be the worst detectives at the agency. At the Foozle home, a new butler is on his way to take up his post when he is attacked and robbed of his uniform by the "Slasher" who is then let into the house by Mrs Foozle, believing him to be the new butler. Stan and Ollie arrive and the Foozles retire to bed. The boys are shown to their room by the butler whom they fail to recognise even after seeing a picture of him in the newspaper. The murderer enters the judge's bedroom, but is scared away by Mrs Foozle's screams. When he hides in the boys' room still brandishing his knife, the penny drops and the three of them end up in a heap on the floor. The "Slasher" chases them down the stairs wielding a huge sword. The judge, dressed in a white sheet, falls down the stairs when startled by his wife's gun accidentally going off. Thinking he has seen a ghost, the "Slasher" drops to his knees in terror. Stan seizes the opportunity and locks him in the closet, which also happens to be Ollie's hiding place. Stan is congratulated for his excellent work as the police arrive to arrest the murderer, with Ollie emerging from the closet sporting two black eyes.

For the first time since DUCK SOUP, the boys were cast together instead of their usual roles as rivals or solo performers. They were

(Stan) 'Well if she didn't go to the mountains, Mohammed would have to come here.'
(SONS OF THE DESERT)

What Was The Film When..?

starting to form identities, which would include the wearing of their shabby, ill-fitting suits and derbies, which would become the customary Laurel and Hardy uniform.

FLYING ELEPHANTS

Directed by **Frank Butler**, Produced by **Hal Roach**, Filmed - May 1927, Released - Feb 12, 1928 by Pathé, Running time - 2 reels.

With: **Stan Laurel** (Little Twinkle Star), **Oliver Hardy** (Mighty Giant), **James Finlayson** (Saxophonus), **Viola Richard** (Blushing Rose), **Leo Willis** (Fisherman), **Dorothy Coburn** (Cavewomen wrestler), **Tiny Sandford, Bud Fine** (Cavemen).

> *"6000 years ago all men were forced to marry or work on the rock pile - That's why it was called the Stone Age."*

It's life in the Stone Age and King Ferdinand, leader of the cave people, decrees that all males between the age of thirteen and ninety-three must marry under threat of banishment, death or both! A mighty giant (Ollie) arrives at the settlement and is informed of the proclamation, but finding a girl not already spoken for is no easy task, something that becomes painfully apparent to him when he gets clubbed over the head by jealous rivals. Little Twinkle Star (Stan), a rather effeminate creature, also hears of the King's wishes and dances joyfully down the mountain in search of true love. He spots Blushing Rose, a pretty young thing, and chases her back to camp where he meets her father, Saxophonus, who is suffering with terrible toothache. Stan is asked of his intentions towards his daughter and how he would provide for her. Stan tells him that he's a fisherman so is asked to prove his ability by catching a whale. He sets off to the river, but his attempts see him accidentally spear another fisherman (Leo Willis) and then club him over the head. Back at camp, Saxophonus has tied a piece of string around the aching molar with the other end fastened to a large rock. Ollie helps by throwing the heavy rock over the edge of the cliff, closely followed by Saxophonus, who is dragged with it. However this does the trick and the troublesome tooth is pulled. Stan returns with his catch of fish, realising that he now has a rival for the girl's affections. Stan and Ollie start a contest for her hand, with Ollie easily winning the encounter, until a mountain goat intervenes and butts him over the edge of the cliff. Stan dances a jig of delight as he claims his prize and

40 Did You Know Clyde Bruckman, credited as director in five Laurel and Hardy silents, committed suicide in a phone booth using a gun borrowed from Buster Keaton.

Cameras Roll, Action!

the sweethearts sit down together. Unfortunately their seat turns out to be a bear, so they make a quick exit with Saxophonus in his cart, as the bear joins them for a free-for-all when the cart tips up.

The final All Star Series film to be distributed by Pathé Exchange. Fed up with being in direct competition with Mack Sennett, Roach signed up with Metro-Goldwyn-Mayer to distribute his films, with Stan and Ollie now given equal star billing. With their films now being shown all over the world, as opposed to the considerably fewer theatres served by Pathé, the move to the world's largest film factory would be a lucrative switch in fortunes for the boys, whose careers were about to take off. Having filmed FLYING ELEPHANTS in May 1927, Pathé sporadically released the remaining films featuring Stan and Ollie throughout that year, with FLYING ELEPHANTS finally released in February 1928, by which time the boys had already appeared in seven MGM distributed films and taken a considerable step up on the ladder to movie stardom.

SUGAR DADDIES

Directed by **Fred Guiol**, Produced by **Hal Roach**, Filmed - Jun 1927, Released - Sep 10, 1927 by MGM, Running time - 2 reels.

With: **James Finlayson** (Cyrus Brittle), **Stan Laurel** (Lawyer), **Oliver Hardy** (Butler), **Charlotte Mineau** ("Wife"), **Noah Young** ("Brother-in-law"), **Edna Marian** ("Step daughter").

Also appeared: Eugene Pallette, Jack Hill, Charlie Hall, Sam Lufkin, Dorothy Coburn, Ray Cooke, Jiggs the dog.

"The story of a millionaire oil man who was married and didn't know it - this will give you a rough idea what oil men are like."

The morning after a boozy night out, millionaire Cyrus Brittle is woken by his butler (Ollie) and horrified to learn that he was married the night before, with the bartender acting as best man. Brittle phones his lawyer (Stan) before going downstairs to meet his new wife, who is accompanied by her brutal looking brother and her daughter. Brittle tries to explain the big mistake but is told to pay $50,000 to get out of his predicament. Stan arrives on the scene and accuses the newcomers of blackmail, but when a pistol is produced by Brittle's new brother-in-law, the millionaire and the boys make a

---

(Title card) The defendant had killed two Chinamen – both seriously (*DO DETECTIVES THINK?*)

quick exit. A week later and still in hiding, Brittle and his entourage hold a riotous party at a swanky hotel that makes the headlines in the newspaper. His brother-in-law reads about the event and storms off to the hotel, where he is spotted in the reception by Stan, who then informs his client. They try to sneak away with Brittle sat on Stan's back, donning a large coat and lady's hat, trying to pass himself off as Ollie's rather tall wife. The unlikely pair leave the hotel closely followed by the blackmailers who are not entirely convinced of the disguise. At a ballroom Ollie takes his "wife" onto the dance floor but they are spotted and chased outside into a fun house at an amusement park. They all descend a huge slide with the pursuers and pursued ending up in a tangled heap at the bottom.

Sam Lufkin (born Utah, 1892) made the first of his 39 appearances in Laurel and Hardy films where he was usually cast in bit-part roles. Roach's move to MGM proved beneficial to both Roach and distributor. It gave MGM some much needed short subjects to show at their chain of movie theatres and meant that Stan and Ollie were now being shown to a larger world wide audience.

THE SECOND HUNDRED YEARS

Directed by **Fred Guiol**, Produced by **Hal Roach**, Edited by **Richard Currier**, Filmed - Jun 1927, Released - Oct 8, 1927 by MGM, Running time - 2 reels.

With: **Frank Brownlee** (Prison warden), **James Finlayson** (Governor Browne Van Dyke), **Tiny Sandford** (Prison guard), **Ellinor Vanderveer** (Countess de Cognac), **Otto Fries** (Lecoque), **Bob O'Conor** (Voitrex).

Also appeared: Eugene Pallette, Edgar Dearing, Charles Bachman, Dorothy Coburn, Rosemary Theby, Charlie Hall, Alfred Fisher.

"Will Rogers says - Being in jail has one big advantage - a man doesn't have to worry about wearing his tuxedo."

Stan (Little Goofy) and Ollie (Big Goofy) are in prison and planning an escape by digging a tunnel underneath their cell. Whilst digging they strike a water pipe so they have to make a detour, only to miscalculate their position and find themselves in the warden's office. With their escape scuppered, they are marching to the canteen when they pass two painters working on the inner walls. The painters leave for lunch so the boys turn their prison uniforms inside out and posing

(Stan to Lola Marcel) 'Now that you've got the mine, I'll bet you'll be a swell gold digger.'
(WAY OUT WEST)

as the workmen, walk through the gates to freedom. On the outside a policeman eyes them suspiciously, so they start to daub everything in sight, including cars, shop windows, lamp posts and even a lady's (Dorothy Coburn) posterior! The boys escape when they jump into a passing limousine and steal the clothes from the passengers, who are thrown onto the street in their underwear. Unfortunately the people in question are French police chiefs, Lecoque and Voitrex, on their way to do a study of the very prison the boys have just escaped from. The car takes Stan and Ollie back to prison where they are escorted to the governor's house as guests of honour at a dinner party. The guests go on a tour of the prison, but when they walk past the cell that houses the French police chiefs, who have been arrested, the boys are immediately recognised and marched back to their cell.

Laurel and Hardy were born! If there had been any doubts in the Roach camp about Stan and Ollie's future as a team, then THE SECOND HUNDRED YEARS, the first of three Laurel and Hardy prison films, laid them to rest. The potential of the team had been noted by Hal Roach and overly encouraged by Leo McCarey. McCarey (born Los Angeles, October 3, 1898) had entered into films in 1918 as an assistant director. By 1926 he had earned the position of Supervisor of Comedy at the Roach Studios, where he would also direct and provide many ideas for Laurel and Hardy storylines. How long Stan and Ollie's team-up would last was uncertain, with Stan keen to return to his real passion of writing and directing. THE SECOND HUNDRED YEARS was the last of Fred Guiol's (born San Francisco, 1898) nine stints in the director's chair.

CALL OF THE CUCKOOS 6

Directed by **Clyde Bruckman**, Produced by **Hal Roach**, Edited by **Richard Currier**, Filmed - Jun 1927, Released - Oct 15, 1927 by MGM, Running time - 2 reels.

With: **Max Davidson** (Papa Gimplewart), **Lillian Elliot** (Mama Gimplewart), **Spec O'Donnell** (Their son), **Stan Laurel, Oliver Hardy, Charley Chase, James Finlayson, Charlie Hall** (Trainee radio announcers), **Leo Willis, Lyle Tayo, Edgar Dearing, Fay Holderness** (Relatives), **Frank Brownlee** (First prospective buyer), **Charles Meakin** (Man in house swap).

(Title card) If we win, we get $100 – If we lose, we get $5 – That's a difference of $1500 *(THE BATTLE OF THE CENTURY)*

Also appeared: Otto Fries.

"There are two kinds of cuckoos - those who live in clocks, and those who can't."

The Gimplewarts' house is up for sale, but they are having trouble finding a buyer due to the crazy antics of their next door neighbours, a group of screwy trainee radio announcers. A prospective buyer turns up to view the property only to be put off by Stan's attempts to shoot an apple off the top of Ollie's head in the garden next door. Not surprisingly he leaves, but it isn't long before they have another customer, offering a straight swap for his rather impressive looking house. A deal is struck, yet on arrival at their new abode, No.1313, the Gimplewarts soon discover that things are not all they seem when Papa Gimplewart switches on the bathroom light and gets a soaking from the shower. Worse follows when gas comes out of the water taps and water out of the stove. The family's relatives turn up for a house warming party and almost demolish the place when a squabble gets out of hand. The piano rolls down the uneven floor, smashing a hole through the wall before wrecking the Gimplewarts' car. Just as it appears nothing else could go wrong, they look through the window and spot their new next door neighbours, none other than the radio announcers who have also moved house.

Hal Roach inserted Stan and Ollie into this Max Davidson short, to publicise the birth of his new found team. They appeared just days after completing THE SECOND HUNDRED YEARS still sporting shaven heads. Publicity stunts such as this would soon be a thing of the past, especially after their next All Star Series film.

HATS OFF

Directed by **Hal Yates**, Produced by **Hal Roach**, Edited by **Richard Currier**, Filmed - Jul/Aug 1927, Released - Nov 5, 1927 by MGM, Running time - 2 reels.

With: **James Finlayson** (Washing machine dealer), **Anita Garvin** (Lady at top of steps), **Dorothy Coburn** (Lady at bottom of steps).

Also appeared: Ham Kinsey, Sam Lufkin, Chet Brandenberg.

"The story of two boys who figure that the world owes them a living - but is about thirty-five years behind in the payments."

Cameras Roll, Action!

Having lost their jobs as dish washers, Stan and Ollie spot a sign advertising for washing machine salesmen. They are hired by the dealer with the job of selling the "Kwickway" washer door-to-door. Driving down the street, they spot a lady waving at them from the top of a large flight of steps. Thinking a sale is possible, they haul the washing machine all the way to the top, only to be asked if they would post a letter for her. To save a wasted journey Ollie asks her if she is interested in buying the product, but is told that she has her own Chinaman to do the washing. The boys, with great effort, lug the machine back down the steps, only for the lady to call them again. Hoping that the Chinaman may have developed back trouble, Ollie sends Stan to investigate. At the top Stan beckons Ollie to follow, so with much huffing and puffing, Ollie again hauls the washer to the top of the steps, this time to be informed that the letter he has taken has no stamp on it. Eventually, back at the bottom their luck seems to change when another lady asks for a demonstration. A sale seems imminent until she tells them where she lives - at the top of the steps!! Frustrations boil over and the dealer arrives as a steamroller crushes the washing machine flat. Ollie knocks off Stan's hat who retaliates by doing the same. Passers-by become involved with everybody's headgear the target for abuse. The police arrest everyone bar Stan and Ollie, who are left sitting amongst the discarded hats.

Despite an extensive and ongoing search, HATS OFF remains the only Laurel and Hardy film to be lost in its entirety. Its loss is mourned by fans and film historians alike, as it was considered one of their best early silent films. Stan's hair, shorn off for the filming of THE SECOND HUNDRED YEARS had now grown back, but stubbornly refused to lay flat during filming. This caused great amusement on the set which Stan took as a huge compliment. His unruly head of hair would be added to the ever growing list of Laurel and Hardy trademarks. The film marked the return of their rag-tag suits and derbies, absent since DO DETECTIVES THINK? A similar storyline to HATS OFF would be used five years later, and would earn Stan and Ollie the highest accolade, when THE MUSIC BOX won an Academy Award for Best Live Action Short Subject of 1931-32. Director Hal Yates would later remake much of HATS OFF with Edgar Kennedy in IT'S YOUR MOVE.

PUTTING PANTS ON PHILIP

Directed by **Clyde Bruckman**, Produced by **Hal Roach**, Edited by **Richard Currier**, Filmed - Aug 1927, Released - Dec 3, 1927 by MGM, Running time - 2 reels.

(Stan as Agnes) 'I mean a half a year. To be exact three months.' *(ANOTHER FINE MESS)*

What Was The Film When..?

With: **Stan Laurel** (Philip), **Oliver Hardy** (Piedmont Mumblethunder), **Sam Lufkin** (Ship's doctor), **Dorothy Coburn** (Pursued victim), **Harvey Clark** (Tailor), **Charles Bachman** (Policeman), **Ed Brandenberg** (Bus conductor).

Also appeared: Chet Brandenberg, Retta Palmer, Bob O'Conor, Eric Mack, Jack Hill, Don Bailey, Alfred Fisher, Lee Phelps.

"The story of a Scotch lad who came to America to hunt for a Columbian half-dollar - his grandfather lost it in 1893."

Piedmont Mumblethunder (Ollie), a gentleman of great distinction, is waiting at the docks for the arrival of his nephew Philip (Stan) from Scotland. He reads a letter from his sister telling him all about his nephew, including his one big weakness - WOMEN! Stan arrives dressed in full Scottish regalia, with his kilt causing much amusement among the dockside crowd. Ollie explains his position in the community and asks Stan to walk several paces behind him, so as not to cause any embarrassment. Stan's strange appearance soon draws a large crowd who start to follow the pair. Stan has to be restrained from chasing an attractive lady (Dorothy Coburn) and provides further entertainment when his kilt billows up after walking over a pavement air vent. Ollie then spots a large crowd gathering, and discovers that Stan is missing. He finds his woman-crazy nephew pursuing his favourite pastime with the same lady who is standing alongside an irate policeman. Ollie promises to resolve the situation by taking Stan to the tailor's shop to have him fitted with a pair of trousers. After a fierce struggle, the tailor finally gets Stan's inside leg measurement and he receives his first ever pair of trousers and goes into the changing cubicle to try them on. There he spots his lady friend walking past the window and in a flash - still minus the trousers - gives chase. Ollie rushes outside and fights his way through the crowd that has gathered, eventually emerging with the romeo and escaping by jumping onto a passing bus. On the top deck Stan sees his lady love and once again Ollie has to save his love-sick nephew from the crowd. Realising he can't win, Ollie decides to introduce Stan to the lady in question, but she isn't at all interested. Stan decides to take the bull by the horns and approaches the lady as she is about to cross the road at a particularly muddy spot. He plays the perfect gentleman by laying his kilt over the muddy patch, and for a moment the lady seems flattered by his noble gesture. That is until she takes a running jump over both muddy patch and Stan's kilt. Ollie sees the funny side of Stan's rebuff and steps onto the kilt himself, only to disappear into the muddy water-hole, to find for once that he is the laughing stock of the crowd.

(Prison Guard) 'What's your name?' (Stan) 'Stanley Laurel.' (Prison Guard) 'Say sir when you're addressing me. Now what's your name?' (Stan) 'Sir Stanley Laurel.' *(PARDON US)*

Cameras Roll, Action!

PUTTING PANTS ON PHILIP was regarded as the first "true" Laurel and Hardy film, although DUCK SOUP, DO DETECTIVES THINK? or THE SECOND HUNDRED YEARS seem to have a better case.

THE BATTLE OF THE CENTURY

Directed by **Clyde Bruckman**, Produced by **Hal Roach**, Edited by **Richard Currier**, Filmed - Sep/Oct 1927, Released - Dec 31, 1927 by MGM, Running time - 2 reels.

With: **Noah Young** ("Thunderclap Callahan"), **Charlie Hall** (Pie delivery man), **Eugene Pallette** (Insurance agent), **Gene Morgan** (Ring announcer), **George French** (Dentist), **Sam Lufkin** (Boxing referee), **Dick Sutherland** (Patient at dentist's), **Anita Garvin** (Lady who slips on pie), **Dick Gilbert** (Sewer worker), **Lyle Tayo** (Lady at window), **Dorothy Coburn** (Lady hit by pie while climbing aboard car), **Charley Young** (Fruit seller).

Also appeared: Al Hallet, Jack Hill, Bob O'Conor, Ham Kinsey, Bert Roach, Ed Brandenberg, Dorothy Walbert, Ellinor Vanderveer, Lou Costello.

"The Big Fight - Ringside seats extended as far west as Honolulu."

Stan is the prize fighter Canvasback Clump, known as "The Human Mop" as he is usually knocked out first punch. His next opponent is a tough mean looking boxer called "Thunderclap Callahan." The fight begins and by a sheer fluke Stan knocks his rival out cold. Callahan's corner men eventually revive their man and send him out for the next round where he promptly lays Stan out flat with a punch so hard that even his manager Ollie faints. When Ollie comes round the stadium is empty and Stan is still curled up fast asleep in the middle of the ring. Next day in the park, an insurance agent sells Ollie an accident policy for his fighter having recognised Stan from the night before. Ollie realises the way to make some money out of Stan is to "arrange" an accident for him and cash in the policy. He strategically places a banana skin on the ground, but his plan backfires when a pie delivery man (Charlie Hall) slips on the skin instead, causing him to spill his tray of pies over the pavement. He notices that Ollie is holding the banana and splats a pie in his face. Ollie retaliates by throwing one back but hits a lady (Dorothy Coburn) as she climbs aboard her car. She in turn hurls one back and hits a gentleman having his shoes shined. Very soon everybody in the neighbourhood has joined in the battle, with pies flying in all directions while Stan supplies the ammunition from the back of the delivery van. The boys leave the scene with the pie fight in full cry. Stan discards his last pie as another lady (Anita Garvin) walks past, slips and sits on it. Stan and Ollie laugh at her misfortune only to arouse the suspicions of a policeman, who asks them if they started the pie fight. *'What pie fight?'* replies Ollie, as the cop gets a wayward pie in the face before chasing them down the street.

Although films involving pie fights had been done many times before, Stan took the idea to Hal Roach to do "a pie fight to end all pie fights." So an entire day's output of 3,000 pies was purchased from The Los Angeles Pie Company to be used during filming. Unfortunately only nine minutes of the film are known to have survived, with about a third of this containing the famous pie fight. One bit-part actor to appear as a crowd extra in the film was Lou Costello. Little did he know that some years later he would be part of a comedy team (Abbott and Costello) which would, in their heyday, be as popular as Stan and Ollie.

LEAVE 'EM LAUGHING

Directed by **Clyde Bruckman**, Produced by **Hal Roach**, Edited by **Richard Currier**, Filmed - Oct 1927, Released - Jan 28, 1928 by MGM, Running Time - 2 reels.

With: **Charlie Hall** (Landlord), **Edgar Kennedy** (Traffic policeman), **Otto Fries** (Dentist pulling Ollie's tooth), **Jack Lloyd** (Dentist), **Dorothy Coburn**, **Viola Richard** (Dental Nurses).

Also appeared: Tiny Sandford, Sam Lufkin, Edgar Dearing, Al Hallet, Jack Hill.

"What's worse than an aching tooth at three in the morning?
TWO OF THEM!"

Ollie is being kept awake by Stan suffering from chronic toothache. When Stan tries to extract the tooth himself it results in the boys clashing with their landlord, who tells them to pack their bags in the morning. Next day Ollie takes his suffering friend to the dentist, though Stan is reluctant to have treatment after witnessing one patient being wheeled out of the surgery

Cameras Roll, Action!

on a stretcher, while another is dragged kicking and screaming into the chair before making his escape. When it comes to Stan's turn he faints, and is carried to the chair before being revived. Ollie hatches a plan with the dentist to creep up and pull the tooth, but the dentist has had enough of the goings-on and hands the job to his assistant (Otto Fries). Back in the surgery, Ollie is in the chair showing Stan how to relax, when the assistant enters and pulls one of Ollie's teeth instead. Ollie tries to man-handle Stan into the chair, but during the struggle they breath in too much gas and are soon laughing uncontrollably. They stagger out to their car where they proceed to bash into several parked cars before running into a traffic jam. A policeman notices their merriment and asks the boys to reverse their car - which they do repeatedly into the car behind them. With the boys still unable to control their chuckles, the cop drives them out of the jam and down a street which is closed for repair and straight into a water hole, with the boys still laughing as they sink from view.

LEAVE 'EM LAUGHING marked the first appearance of Edgar Kennedy in a Laurel and Hardy film along with the boys' faithful Model T Ford, affectionately known as a "Tin Lizzy," which would be scrapped, squashed, blown-up and even sawn in half in future films.

THE FINISHING TOUCH

Directed by **Clyde Bruckman**, Produced by **Hal Roach**, Edited by **Richard Currier**, Filmed - Nov/Dec 1927, Released - Feb 25, 1928 by MGM, Running time - 2 reels.

With: **Sam Lufkin** (House owner), **Edgar Kennedy** (Policeman), **Dorothy Coburn** (Nurse).

"The story of two boys who went to school for nine years - and finished in the first reader."

Stan and Ollie are carpenters, approached by the owner of a half-built house, who promises them $500 if they can finish off the job by noon the following Monday. Ollie is so impressed by the offer, he promises the job will be completed by noon that very day. They set to work, but across the road a nurse complains to a passing policeman that the noise coming from the building site is upsetting the patients in the hospital. The boys are told to keep quiet, to no avail as Ollie crashes through a door he is carrying because Stan removes the wooden plank he is using as a ramp. Standing on another plank, Ollie sets about the task of gluing the roof tiles,

---
(Title card) Her brother - Has three bad habits - He steals things - He kills people - and he eats with his knife (*SUGAR DADDIES*)

but Stan saws it in half, and Ollie covers the unfortunate policeman with glue and tiles. Unbelievably the house is finished on time, with the owner delighted with the finished article. As he hands over the money for a job well done, a small bird lands on the chimney stack that collapses under its weight, followed closely by the porch railings and window frames. The owner demands his money back with the boys reluctant to hand it over. Ollie hurls a bucket of whitewash at him, which covers the policeman, returning to the site after changing into a fresh uniform. A rock throwing battle breaks out, and a stray stone knocks the nurse into a trough of whitewash. Stan and Ollie then grapple over a large rock they both want to throw, unaware that this is all that's preventing their truck from rolling down the hill. The warring trio stop to witness the vehicle trundle down the slope and complete the house demolition.

The film was based loosely on the Stan Laurel solo SMITHY.

FROM SOUP TO NUTS

Directed by **E. Livingston Kennedy**, Produced by **Hal Roach**, Edited by **Richard Currier**, Filmed - Dec 1927/Jan 1928, Released - Mar 24, 1928 by MGM, Running time - 2 reels.

With: **Anita Garvin** (Mrs Culpepper), **Tiny Sandford** (Mr. Culpepper), **Edna Marian** (Maid), **Otto Fries** (Chef), **Ellinor Vanderveer** (Arrogant dinner guest).

Also appeared: George Bichel, Dorothy Coburn, Sam Lufkin, Gene Morgan, Buddy the dog.

"Mrs Culpepper is an idol to the snobs - and a pain in the neck to everybody else."

A wealthy couple - Mr. and Mrs Culpepper - are holding a grand dinner party with Stan and Ollie hired as waiters - the best the employment agency could come up with at such short notice. They report to the kitchen, where Stan and the chef are soon smashing plates over each other's heads. The party begins and Ollie enters the dining room carrying a large cream cake, only to slip on a discarded banana skin and dive head first into the cake. He throws the skin away and Stan slips on it, covering the host in soup. Stan also discards the skin for Ollie to dive headlong into a second cream cake. Ollie returns with a third cake, this time on a trolley. The hostess asks him to serve the salad

Cameras Roll, Action!

"without dressing" so, slightly bemused by the request, he instructs Stan to serve the salad "undressed," which he does in his underwear! This causes uproar among the guests, and with the party ruined, the hostess socks Ollie, sending him sprawling into the cake.

Making the first of his two stints in the director's chair was Edgar Livingston Kennedy (born California, April 26, 1890), who would also appear in nine Laurel and Hardy films, proving to be their fiercest on-screen opponent. The cocktail cherry chasing-around-the-plate episode performed by Stan in THE SECOND HUNDRED YEARS, was repeated in FROM SOUP TO NUTS by Anita Garvin. Ollie, who had been appearing in other Roach films, would not make another one without Stan until 1939, due to the phenomenal rise in popularity of Laurel and Hardy.

YOU'RE DARN TOOTIN'

Directed by **E. Livingston Kennedy**, Produced by **Hal Roach**, Edited by **Richard Currier**, Filmed - Jan 1928, Released - Apr 21, 1928 by MGM, Running time - 2 reels.

With: **Otto Lederer** (Band leader), **Agnes Steele** (Landlady, Sister McPherson), **Sam Lufkin** (Diner), **Christian Frank** (Policeman), **Chet Brandenberg** (Worker in man hole), **Rolfe Sedan** (Drunkard), **George Rowe** (Cross-eyed passer by).

Also appeared: Ham Kinsey, William Irving, Charlie Hall, Dick Gilbert, Frank Saputo.

"The story of two musicians who played neither by note nor ear - they used brute strength."

Stan plays clarinet and Ollie the French horn in the municipal band. When they ruin the band leader's farewell concert in the park they are sacked. Returning to their boarding house for dinner, Stan finds a note on the table informing them that they owe fourteen weeks rent. Unconcerned by this they continue their meal until a small boy, also present at the concert in the park, tells the landlady that the boys are now redundant, so they are ordered to leave. To earn themselves some cash, the boys take to street busking, where a policeman spots their act and tells them to move on. Further down the street they set up again, unaware that the band leader is holding another farewell concert in an apartment above the spot

---
Did You Know Ollie's attempts at following in his father's military footsteps were thwarted by his obvious bulk, when he was turned away at the recruiting office during the Great War of 1914-18.

Edgar Kennedy
1890 - 1948

Cameras Roll, Action!

where they are playing. Their performance is so bad that the angry band leader throws a bucket of water at them, but soaks the policeman who is moving them on again. Outside a restaurant they strike up once more, with Ollie blaming their lack of success on Stan's poor musical ability, and shows his frustrations by snapping Stan's clarinet in half. Not to be outdone, Stan kicks the French horn into the street where it is squashed flat by a steamroller. They swap blows before a diner (Sam Lufkin) leaving the restaurant also joins in the squabble. Passers-by are drawn into the fray, and a shin-kicking, trouser-ripping episode breaks out, with everybody soon trouserless. A policeman goes over to sort out the situation and is promptly relieved of his pants by Stan. The boys then jump into a single pair of large trousers "loaned" from a rather portly gentleman, and make their getaway.

Released in Britain as THE MUSIC BLASTERS.

THEIR PURPLE MOMENT

Directed by **James Parrott**, Produced by **Hal Roach**, Edited by **Richard Currier**, Filmed - Feb/Mar 1928, Released - May 19, 1928 by MGM, Running time - 2 reels.

With: **Fay Holderness** (Stan's wife, Mrs Pincher), **Lyle Tayo** (Ollie's wife), **Kay Deslys** (Stan's date), **Anita Garvin** (Ollie's date), **Tiny Sandford** (Head waiter), **Leo Willis** (Cab driver), **Sam Lufkin** (Waiter), **Harry Earles** (Cabaret star), **Patsy O'Byrne** ("Gossip"), **Jimmy Aubrey** (Chef), **Jack Hill** (Doorman), **Ed Brandenberg** (Waiter), **Dorothy Walbert** (Waitress).

Also appeared: Retta Palmer.

"Dedicated to husbands who 'hold out' part of the pay envelope on their wives - and live to tell about it."

The boys plan a night out away from their nagging wives with money Stan has secretly stashed away. However his wife discovers the hoard hidden inside a picture and replaces it with a bundle of worthless cigar coupons. The unsuspecting husbands inform their wives of their trip to the bowling alley, only to head off into town, calling in at the Pink Pup club instead. They team up with two ladies, whose dates have been turfed out for not being able to pay the bill. The foursome order steaks with all the trimmings and settle down to enjoy the cabaret. Stan is so impressed by a troupe of marching midgets that he buys them all a box of candy. When asked to pay, he discovers the coupons, and to make matters worse, a cab driver confronts him demanding payment of the girls' ever-spiralling bill. Ollie, still unaware of the problem, asks the cabby to join them and orders another steak. When Ollie finds out the truth, they try to sneak out of the club but are foiled by the burly head waiter, who is now wise to their financial plight. The boys' wives then arrive on the scene, so Stan and Ollie run into the kitchens. Ollie tries to save his own skin by telling his wife that Stan had dragged him into the club while on the way to the bowling alley. Annoyed by this accusation, Stan hurls a pie but splats Ollie's wife instead. As usual things get out of hand, and a battle ensues involving pie fillings, eggs and bowls of soup.

The mis-match of Stan and Ollie versus shrewd and crafty wives, would be repeated many times in subsequent films. Directed by James Parrott (born Baltimore, 1897), who was Charley Chase's younger brother. He would work with the boys until 1933, directing them through what was considered the golden era of their careers.

SHOULD MARRIED MEN GO HOME?

Directed by **James Parrott**, Produced by **Hal Roach**, Edited by **Richard Currier**, Filmed - Mar-May 1928, Released - Sep 8, 1928 by MGM, Running time - 2 reels.

With: **Edgar Kennedy** (Impatient golfer), **Kay Deslys** (Mrs Hardy), **Edna Marian** (Blonde golfer), **Viola Richard** (Brunette golfer), **Charlie Hall** (Soda fountain attendant), **John Aassen** (Giant), **Sam Lufkin** (Golf shop attendant), **Chet Brandenberg** (Caddie).

Also appeared: Jack Hill, Dorothy Coburn, Lyle Tayo.

"Question - What is the surest way to keep a husband home?
Answer - Break both his legs."

For once the Hardys are enjoying a peaceful morning at home together, until their moment of bliss is interrupted when Stan visits dressed in his golf togs. Despite not being at all interested in playing, Ollie is ordered out of the house after Stan ruins the window shutter and a chair, with Ollie himself demolishing the record player. At the golf course they team up with two lady golfers (Edna Marian and Viola Richard) and head for the soda fountain for a pre-match drink. With only 15 cents between them, the boys

Cameras Roll, Action!

devise a plan for Ollie to order the drinks and Stan to refuse when asked. Stan has trouble grasping the idea and keeps ordering, so when the bill amounts to 30 cents, he has to hand over his watch to cover the bill. On the first tee they become involved with an impatient player (Edgar Kennedy) who fires his ball into a large muddy pool. Stan shows him the rule card stating that the ball must be played from where it lands. Kennedy wades into the water and attempts to hit the ball, but his erratic swing sends clumps of mud flying in all directions, splattering a lady golfer. She flings a handful of mud back, only to hit Ollie's playing partner (Viola Richard) instead and before long a full scale mud battle breaks out. Ollie ends up in the muddy pool and is soon joined by Stan when an 8' 9" giant becomes involved in the rumpus. The boys then realise they are sitting on somebody, as Kennedy emerges with a smile on his face having found his lost ball.

Ollie's true life obsession was golf, and while Stan would stay behind at the studios perfecting a gag or storyline, Ollie, a low handicapper (and regular winner of the Roach Studios golf tournaments), would invariably be found on the course pursuing his passion. SHOULD MARRIED MEN GO HOME? became the first Laurel and Hardy Series film.

EARLY TO BED

Directed by **Emmett Flynn**, Produced by **Hal Roach**, Edited by **Richard Currier**, Filmed - May 1928, Released - Oct 6, 1928 by MGM, Running time - 2 reels.

With: Buster the dog.

"9 a.m. to 10 a.m. That important hour when financial kings of the world open their mail."

Again the boys are down on their luck, and spending the morning in the park with their pet dog. Ollie opens his mail to learn that he's inherited a fortune from his uncle, so offers Stan a job as his butler. At the Hardy mansion, Stan settles down to his duties, where one evening, Ollie arrives home the worse for wear after a day out drinking champagne. Stan tries to get him to go to bed but Ollie, still in a playful mood, won't have any of it unless Stan can catch him. Stan has soon had enough of his master's tomfoolery and retires himself, only to be woken by Ollie pouring water into the bed. This is the final straw, and Stan tells him that he is quitting in the

---

(Title card) Purser Cryder had only two things on his mind – blondes and brunettes
(SAILORS, BEWARE!)

(Top) Movie history is made with Stan and Ollie's first on screen meeting in THE LUCKY DOG and below, Stan and Anita Garvin (far right) in SAILORS, BEWARE!

Anita Garvin in menacing mood in THEIR PURPLE MOMENT

What Was The Film When..?

(Top) A prelude to THE BATTLE OF THE CENTURY in THEIR PURPLE MOMENT and (below) Sam Lufkin gives Stan the once over in PUTTING PANTS ON PHILIP

Cameras Roll, Action!

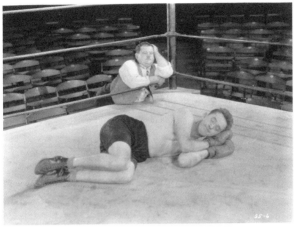

(Top) Ollie despairs with his prize fighter in THE BATTLE OF THE CENTURY, while (below) Anita Garvin provides further heartache for the boys in the sadly lost HATS OFF

What Was The Film When..?

(Top) The boys paint the town white in THE SECOND HUNDRED YEARS while (below) Ollie plans to "play around" in SHOULD MARRIED MEN GO HOME?

Cameras Roll, Action!

FROM SOUP TO NUTS with Anita Garvin

Edgar Kennedy in THE FINISHING TOUCH

morning. Next day with bags packed, Stan hands Ollie the bill for services rendered, but it is refused point blank. In a fit of temper, Stan goes on the rampage, smashing everything in sight before falling head first into a large cream cake. When Ollie confronts him over the damage, he notices the cream on Stan's face and thinks he's frothing at the mouth and has gone mad. Ollie hides in an ornamental fountain, disguising himself as a water-spouting gargoyle. However he can't keep up the ruse for long and bursts out laughing. Stan eventually sees the funny side and decides to forgive his friend, only to be pushed into the fountain.

The fountain sketch at the end of the film had been previously done in the Oliver Hardy short SHOULD MEN WALK HOME? One of only two regular Laurel and Hardy films where the boys are the sole performers (apart from Buster the dog!).

TWO TARS

Directed by **James Parrott**, Produced by **Hal Roach**, Edited by **Richard Currier**, Filmed - Jun/Jul 1928, Released - Nov 3, 1928 by MGM, Running time - 2 reels.

With: Edgar Kennedy (Burned up motorist), **Thelma Hill** (Ollie's date, Thelma), **Ruby Blaine** (Stan's date, Ruby), **Charlie Hall** (Drug store worker), **Thomas Roberts** (First tomato thrower), **Edgar Dearing** (Motorbike cop), **Clara Guiol** (Kennedy's passenger), **Harry Bernard** (Trucker in tomato fight), **Sam Lufkin** (Reading newspaper by lamp post).

Also appeared: Charley Rogers, Jack Hill, Baldwin Cooke, Charles McMurphy, Ham Kinsey, Lyle Tayo, Lon Poff, Retta Palmer, Chet Brandenberg, George Rowe, Fred Holmes, Dorothy Walbert, Frank Ellis, Helen Gilmore.

"Our Navy - Japan - China - The Philippines - And now, the good old U.S.A."

Stan and Ollie are sailors on shore leave from the battleship *Oregon*. Determined to make the most of their day, they hire a car and pick up two girls after helping them with a troublesome

Cameras Roll, Action!

bubble gum machine outside a drug store. They head off into the countryside where, after a fun filled day, they run into a massive traffic jam. With tempers already running high, the boys' arrival only makes things worse, especially when another motorist (Edgar Kennedy) crashes into the back of their car. A fighting and wrecking spree breaks out, with the disorder witnessed by a passing motorbike cop. He asks who started the trouble, and with all fingers pointing at Stan and Ollie, they are placed under arrest. The cop sorts out the jam and the cars move off, some minus wheels, others without roofs and one even moves off upside down! Stan and Ollie are told to follow the cop to jail, but make their getaway when a large truck squashes the policeman's motorbike flat. The rest of the cars are ordered to give chase, with the procession following the boys into a railway tunnel, before quickly reversing out as a train enters at the other end. The boys however are not so fortunate and emerge from the tunnel in a sorry state.

Baldwin Cooke (born New York, 1888), one of Stan's former vaudeville partners in The Stan Jefferson Trio, made his Laurel and Hardy debut in TWO TARS, along with Harry Bernard (born San Francisco, 1878). Between them they would make over 50 appearances with the boys.

HABEAS CORPUS 7

Directed by **James Parrott**, Produced by **Hal Roach**, Edited by **Richard Currier**, Filmed - Jul 1928, Released - Dec 1, 1928 by MGM, Running time - 2 reels.

With: **Richard Carle** (Professor Padilla), **Charley Rogers** (Butler and undercover cop, Ledoux), **Charles Bachman** (Policeman).

"Professor Padilla expected to startle the medical world with his new theory - that the human brain has a level surface - in some instances, practically flat."

A mad professor needs a body for his experiments, so when the boys go begging at his home, he offers them the job of stealing a corpse from the graveyard. However, the police have been observing his work, with Ledoux the butler really an undercover cop. Ledoux telephones the information to the police chief, who instructs him to follow the boys to the graveyard, while he goes to arrest the

What Was The Film When..?

professor. Armed with a shovel, lamp and body bag, Stan and Ollie arrive at the cemetery. Stan starts to dig, but is scared off by Ledoux dressed in a white sheet, who jumps into the newly dug grave and climbs inside the bag before Stan returns, picks it up, and slings it over his shoulder. When the "corpse" tips Ollie's hat, the boys make a run for it, with Ollie falling into a water filled hole in the road. Stan leaps over the hole but Ledoux falls out of the bag and into the water. He emerges still covered in the sheet and the boys make a quick exit.

The release date for HABEAS CORPUS was delayed while Hal Roach toyed with the idea of using synchronised music and sound effects. It became the first Laurel and Hardy film to benefit. The actual switch to talking pictures though, was still a further eight films away.

WE FAW DOWN

Directed by **Leo McCarey**, Produced by **Hal Roach**, Edited by **Richard Currier**, Filmed - Aug/Sep 1928, Released - Dec 29, 1928 by MGM, Running time - 2 reels.

With: **Vivien Oakland** (Mrs Hardy), **Bess Flowers** (Mrs Laurel), **Kay Deslys** (Boxer's girlfriend), **Vera White** (Kay's girlfriend), **George Kotsonaros** ("One-Round Kelly"), **Allen Cavan** (Pedestrian).

"This story is based upon the assumption that, somewhere in the world, there are husbands who do not tell their wives everything."

The Laurels and the Hardys are at home together. The boys have been invited to a poker game and are trying to think up an excuse to get out of the house. When they receive a phone call enquiring of their whereabouts, Ollie pretends that it's his boss inviting them out for a night at the Orpheum Theatre. On the way to the poker game, they help recover a lady's hat that has blown underneath a parked car, only to be rewarded for their gallantry with a soaking from a passing street cleaning truck. The grateful owner of the hat (Kay Deslys) invites them up to her apartment to dry their clothes, while back at home the wives read with horror the newspaper headlines -ORPHEUM THEATRE BURNS - and rush round to the scene. At the apartment the boys are enjoying a beer with the lady and her girlfriend and are soon "soaked" both inside and out. The lady takes quite a shine to Stan, blowing him kisses and ruffling his hair, but Stan isn't too impressed with the attention he is receiving and complains to Ollie

(Stan to Ollie) 'Good now you can take a nice hot bath and relapse, and the doctor wont have to give you a continental...' *(SAPS AT SEA)*

Cameras Roll, Action!

that she is too fat. This doesn't go down well and Stan is chased around the table before Ollie intervenes and holds her off, just as her tough boyfriend "One-Round Kelly" enters the room. He pulls a knife on Ollie but Stan saves the day when he splats a cream cake into the boxer's face. This gives them enough time to gather their clothes and escape through the window, all of which is witnessed by their wives who just happen to be passing. The boys arrive home and Ollie receives the third degree from Mrs Hardy who is keen to know about the show they supposed to have seen. In desperation Stan tries to mime the name of the acts from the newspaper, with Ollie's attempts at interpreting them failing miserably. Stan then notices the headlines about the fire and realises the game is up, while Ollie tries to save face by telling his wife that they have been to the Palace Theatre instead. To make matters worse, the lady's girlfriend calls with Ollie's waistcoat, so Mrs Hardy armed with a shotgun, runs the boys out of the house. She fires at them as they run between apartment blocks, sending scores of half-dressed men jumping from every window.

Leo McCarey, arguably the man responsible for the evolution of the Laurel and Hardy partnership, was promoted from his usual role of supervisor to that of director. He would also be in the chair for LIBERTY and WRONG AGAIN. WE FAW DOWN was released in Britain under the slightly different title WE SLIP UP.

LIBERTY

Directed by **Leo McCarey**, Produced by **Hal Roach**, Edited by **Richard Currier & William Terhune**, Filmed - Oct/Nov 1928, Released - Jan 26, 1929 by MGM, Running time - 2 reels.

With: **James Finlayson** (Music store assistant), **Harry Bernard** (Fish shop worker), **Ed Brandenberg** (Cab driver), **Jean Harlow** (Lady getting into cab), **Tom Kennedy** (Chasing prison guard), **Jack Hill** (Policeman), **Sam Lufkin** (Passenger in getaway car), **Jack Raymond** (Driver of getaway car).

"The cradle of American history is rocked by the memory of it's heroes who fought for Liberty - 1777-1778 - Washington suffered privation at Valley Forge in his long fight for freedom - liberty - 1863 - Lincoln said 'A nation conceived in liberty' - 1917 - Pershing led his forces across the sea - And even today - the fight for liberty continues."

What Was The Film When..?

The boys are escaped convicts being chased by a prison guard. They are picked up by friends in a getaway car and change out of their prison uniforms, before being dropped off in the street. In their rush to get changed, they have put on each other's trousers, so try to find a suitable place to swap them back. They are disturbed behind a fishmonger's shop, with Stan quickly pulling up the trousers, oblivious to the fact that a crab has fallen into the seat of his pants. The crab causes Stan to startle Ollie, who knocks over a pile of records outside a music store. They hurry away to a building site where they again try to do the exchange, this time in an elevator. Whilst attempting to change, Ollie accidentally knocks the "up" switch and they rise to the top of a partially built skyscraper. They become stranded when they step out and the lift returns to the ground. Eventually they accomplish the task with Ollie now having the crab as company. They spot a ladder on the other side of the building and somehow reach it, despite the crab nipping Ollie whilst they're precariously balanced on the steel girders. Ollie discovers the crab, just as the ladder and a sandbag fall from the building, narrowly missing a policeman standing below. The elevator returns to the top allowing them to descend safely, and crush the policeman who has taken shelter from the falling debris in the elevator shaft. The boys flee with the cop emerging from his ordeal as a midget.

LIBERTY was written using excess material from WE FAW DOWN. Among the bit-part players was an attractive platinum-blonde, Harlean Carpenter, who would be better known by her stage name of Jean Harlow. She would also appear in DOUBLE WHOOPEE and BACON GRABBERS before going on to become a big movie star in her own right.

WRONG AGAIN

Directed by **Leo McCarey**, Produced by **Hal Roach**, Edited by **Richard Currier**, Filmed - Nov/Dec 1928, Released - Feb 23, 1929 by MGM, Running time - 2 reels.

With: **Del Henderson** (Millionaire), **Josephine Crowell** (His mother), **Harry Bernard** (Policeman), **Fred Holmes** (Stable hand), **William Gillespie** (Stable owner), **Sam Lufkin** (Detective Sullivan), **Jack Hill** (Man in buggy which loses wheel), **Charlie Hall** (Neighbour).

"At the fashionable Piping Rock Riding Academy."

Cameras Roll, Action!

Stable hands Stan and Ollie are cleaning out the stall belonging to a horse named Blue Boy, when they overhear that Blue Boy has been stolen and its millionaire owner is offering a $5,000 reward for its return. The boys are soon on their way to his home with the horse in tow, not knowing that the "Blue Boy" in question is the famous Gainsborough painting. The thieves are soon caught, and the millionaire is informed over the telephone that the prized painting will be returned as soon as possible. Stan and Ollie arrive at his mansion just as he is about to take a bath. Thinking they are the detectives, he throws down the keys and tells the boys to take Blue Boy into the house. Although this seems a strange request, Ollie explains to Stan that all aristocrats are a bit eccentric, and as if to prove Ollie right, the owner shouts down the stairs to put Blue Boy on top of the piano. The boys set about the task, and only after a great deal of effort and coaxing do they manage to get the horse onto the piano. The millionaire's mother arrives with the detectives and the painting, leaving the owner demanding to know what the boys have brought into the house. When the horse is led out, the owner has to be restrained by the detectives and in the ensuing struggle the painting is ruined. The boys and the horse are chased from the estate by the incensed millionaire armed with his shotgun. He is escorted back to the house by a less-than-happy policeman, who has the seat of his trousers smouldering.

THAT'S MY WIFE

Directed by **Lloyd French**, Produced by **Hal Roach**, Edited by **Richard Currier**, Filmed - Dec 1928, Released - Mar 23, 1929 by MGM, Running time - 2 reels.

With: **Vivien Oakland** (Mrs Hardy), **William Courtwright** (Uncle Bernal), **Jimmy Aubrey** (Drunkard), **Harry Bernard** (Thieving waiter), **Charlie Hall** (Waiter), **Sam Lufkin** (Waiter who falls in the cake).

"Mr. Hardy's house had become less and less a home since Mr. Laurel joined the family."

The Hardy household has not been a happy one since Stan became the permanent lodger. In fact things get so bad that Mrs Hardy leaves home. Ollie's Uncle Bernal arrives in town, promising his nephew a large inheritance as long as he can prove that he's still happily married. Faced with this dilemma, Ollie persuades Stan to dress up and masquerade as his wife. Stan reluctantly agrees, and donning a dress and doll's wig, is introduced as "Magnolia," making a less-than-dignified entrance, down the stairs on his backside after

---

(Ollie) 'Why it's too far fetched not to be the truth isn't it Stanley.' (Stan) 'It's imposterous.'
(SONS OF THE DESERT)

having trouble walking on his high heels. Uncle Bernal takes them to the Pink Pup club for dinner, where Stan plays such a convincing role that a drunkard joins them at the table, openly flirting with Stan. Uncle Bernal orders Ollie to sort out the situation, so he obliges by pouring soup over the drunk's head, who then leaves requesting his bill and a bowl of soup "to take out." Stan then notices a waiter stealing a necklace from an unsuspecting lady customer. The theft is discovered and the manager promises that everybody will be searched. In a panic the thief drops the necklace down the back of Stan's dress, so Ollie tries to retrieve it by shaking Stan up and down on the dance floor. They continue the search in a phone booth, not knowing that the necklace has fallen out and been handed back to the owner. The cabaret begins and as the curtain opens, it reveals Stan and Ollie on all fours, still looking for the necklace. As the boys are confronted by Uncle Bernal, they slip over causing Stan to lose his wig and blow the charade. Uncle Bernal leaves, promising his fortune to the cats and dogs hospital. Ollie then suffers further humiliation when the drunkard pours soup over his head.

Jimmy Aubrey (born Bolton, England in 1889) who played the drunk, was an old associate of Stan and Ollie's, having worked with Stan during his Fred Karno days and Ollie in a series of films at Vitagraph.

BIG BUSINESS

Directed by **James Horne**, Produced by **Hal Roach**, Edited by **Richard Currier**, Filmed - Dec 1928, Released - Apr 20, 1929 by MGM, Running time - 2 reels.

With: **James Finlayson** (Irate customer), **Tiny Sandford** (Policeman).

Also appeared: Lyle Tayo, Retta Palmer, Charlie Hall.

*"The story of a man who turned the other cheek
- and got punched in the nose."*

Business is not good for the boys selling Christmas trees to the residents of sunny California. They call at one particular house only to have its owner (James Finlayson) slam the door in their faces, trapping the top of the tree in the process. They knock a

Cameras Roll, Action!

James Finlayson
1887 - 1953

second time and the same thing happens, firstly trapping the tree and then Stan's overcoat. This occurs several more times before the owner loses his temper and chops the tree into pieces with a pair of garden shears. Stan's retribution is to take out his pen knife and carve chunks out of the door surround. Very soon tit-for-tat warfare develops, with the wrathful house owner venting his anger on the boys' car, while Stan and Ollie rip up plants, chop down trees and break the house windows. A policeman witnesses the destruction while Ollie smashes vases "baseball style" as Stan pitches them through the window. Ollie only stops after breaking one that has come to rest on the policeman's foot. Stan, still unaware of the policeman's presence, drags a piano into the garden and chops it up, as their combatant wrestles on the floor with dismembered Christmas trees. The policeman calls the warring parties together, and before long they have settled their differences and made up. To show there are no hard feelings, Stan hands their new friend a cigar, which when lit, explodes in his face.

It is hard to say which was Stan and Ollie's best silent film. Most film critics and Laurel and Hardy stalwarts would probably award the honour to either BIG BUSINESS or TWO TARS, both films with the emphasis on mass destruction.

DOUBLE WHOOPEE

Directed by **Lewis Foster**, Produced by **Hal Roach**, Edited by **Richard Currier**, Filmed - Feb 1929, Released - May 18, 1929 by MGM, Running time - 2 reels.

With: **Captain John Peters** (Visiting Prince), **Tiny Sandford** (Policeman), **Charlie Hall** (Annoyed cab driver), **Jean Harlow** (Lady who loses her dress), **William Gillespie** (Hotel manager), **Rolfe Sedan** (Desk clerk), **Charley Rogers** (Prime Minister), **Sam Lufkin** (Man poked in the eye), **Ed Brandenberg** (Bellhop), **Ham Kinsey** (Cab driver).

"Broadway - street of a thousand thrills."

A large Broadway hotel is busy preparing for the arrival of a foreign Prince. The royal car draws up, and as the manager and the staff wait for the Prince's entrance, Stan and Ollie

Cameras Roll, Action!

arrive to take up their positions as doorman and footman. At first they are mistaken for the royal visitors, but when the real Prince and his entourage enter, the boys are ordered to change into their uniforms. On the way up to his suite, the royal guest, with just a little help from Stan and Ollie, manages to fall down a mud-filled lift shaft, not once but twice! He goes to change his ruined uniform as Ollie begins his door duties, where he is soon joined outside by Stan, who is unable to help himself when he spots a whistle on Ollie's tunic. This immediately summons a taxi to the door, with the cab driver less than happy about his wasted journey, showing his anger by ripping Ollie's uniform to bits. A pretty lady guest (Jean Harlow) draws up at the hotel, but as she steps out, Stan slams the taxi door and traps her dress, which is ripped off her back, when Ollie escorts her to reception. Stan is made to take off his coat to cover the lady's blushes, leaving him standing in just his underwear and top hat. The boys begin to argue with the manager and a number of guests also caught up in the disagreement, which turns into a full scale brawl. The boys are given their marching orders and head upstairs to pack their bags. Meanwhile the fight continues, with a waiter spilling a large cream cake over the Prince as he descends the stairs. On the way back up to his suite - to change yet again - he falls down the lift shaft for a third time, as the elevator is summoned by the boys, who with bags packed, are leaving.

Directed by Lewis Foster, who would be in the chair for the next six Laurel and Hardy films, including the big switch to "talkies."

BACON GRABBERS

Directed by **Lewis Foster**, Produced by **Hal Roach**, Edited by **Richard Currier**, Filmed - Feb-Mar 1929, Released - Oct 19, 1929 by MGM, Running time - 2 reels.

With: **Edgar Kennedy** (Collis P. Kennedy), **Charlie Hall** (Truck driver), **Harry Bernard** (Policeman), **Jean Harlow** (Mrs Kennedy), **Eddie Baker** (Sheriff), **Bobby Dunn** (Building site worker), **Sam Lufkin** (Man who delivers attachment papers).

Also appeared: Buddy the dog.

"The Northwest Mounties always get their man - but - The Attachment Squad of The Sheriff's office get everything from a grand piano to the Grand Canyon."

(Ollie) 'What are you doing?' (Stan) 'Someone's knocking on the phone.'
(Ollie) 'That's levity.' (Stan) 'Hello Mr. Levity.' *(BEAU HUNKS)*

What Was The Film When..?

(Top) The game is up for the boys in WE FAW DOWN and a similar fate awaits them (below) in THAT'S MY WIFE

Cameras Roll, Action!

The platinum blonde bombshell Jean Harlow in DOUBLE WHOOPEE

What Was The Film When..?

Repossession officers Stan and Ollie, are working for the sheriffs' office, and are given the job of retrieving a radio from a Collis P. Kennedy, a very tough customer, who hasn't paid an instalment on the radio since 1921. Their initial attempt to serve the order fails when Kennedy scares the boys away with a lifelike toy dog. Ollie borrows a large dog from a small boy, but the toy scares it so much, it drags Ollie down the path and across the road. Eventually they manage to serve the papers, but Kennedy challenges them to try and get the radio as he goes back into the house. They attempt to gain entry through an upstairs window, but Kennedy is one step ahead and repels their efforts using his shotgun. Fortunately for the boys his aim is poor and he hits a fire hydrant instead, soaking a passing policeman. The cop investigates and orders Kennedy to hand over the radio as he rings the station requesting a wagon. Stan and Ollie emerge triumphantly from the house with the goods and a fight breaks out, with the radio left in the middle of the road, where it gets flattened by a steamroller. Kennedy cannot hide his joy as he shouts *'There's your radio, try an' get Havana.'* At this point he is joined by his wife who proudly produces a receipt and informs him that she has paid for the radio in full, and it is now legally theirs. This time it's the boys' turn to laugh, but this too is short lived as the steamroller continues down the street and crushes their car.

BACON GRABBERS, based on an old Fred Karno skit became another casualty of the talking picture revolution and gathered dust until eventually being released after the boys had already established themselves in "talkies," with five pictures already doing the rounds.

ANGORA LOVE

Directed by **Lewis Foster**, Produced by **Hal Roach**, Edited by **Richard Currier**, Filmed - Mar 1929, Released - Dec 14, 1929 by MGM, Running time - 2 reels.

With: **Edgar Kennedy** (Landlord), **Charlie Hall** (Hotel guest), **Harry Bernard** (Policeman), **Charley Young** (Mr. Caribeau).

"The dramatic story of a goat - a strong dramatic story."

When Penelope the goat breaks her tether outside the pet shop, her owner Mr. Caribeau, fears the worst and informs the police that the goat has been stolen. Stan and

---

(Landlord) 'What kind of a room do you want?' (Ollie) 'We'd like to see your floor plan please.'
(Landlord) 'Floor plan?' (Stan) 'Yes sir, we'd like a room with a southern explosion.' *(ANY OLD PORT)*

Ollie run into her outside a confectionery shop having just spent their last dime on doughnuts, with Stan making the mistake of feeding some to the affectionate goat, who then starts to follow. When they hear that the goat has been stolen, the boys run off, fearful of a long stretch in prison for "kid"napping. Two nights later and with Penelope still in tow, they decide to hide her in their rented room. After smuggling her past their strict landlord, the boys decide to give her a bath, to get rid it of the pungent smell. However, the bath water spills and seeps through the floorboards onto the sleeping landlord in the room below. He rings the police telling them that there is going to be a murder, before walking into the boys' room to find them hard at work shampooing the goat. Stan spots the landlord and in a panic shoves Ollie's head in the suds. Ollie picks up the tin bath and hurls the contents at Stan, who ducks, and it's the landlord who gets the soaking. A water fight breaks out between Ollie and the landlord, with a policeman arriving just in time to receive a drenching as well. The cop then notices Penelope sitting quietly in the corner, and accuses the landlord of the theft. Wet, exhausted and wishing never to set eyes on another goat again, the boys sit down as three kid goats emerge from underneath the bed.

This was to be their last regular silent picture and was not seen until at least eight months after filming, by which time six Laurel and Hardy talking shorts had already been released. ANGORA LOVE provided the ideas for LAUGHING GRAVY (1931) and THE CHIMP (1932), as well as sketches for BE BIG (1931) and BEAU HUNKS (1931).

What Was The Film When..?

Anita Garvin looks on as Stan and Edna Marian become familiar in FROM SOUP TO NUTS

Any Nuts?
The Talking Pictures

Any Nuts?

UNACCUSTOMED AS WE ARE

Directed by **Lewis Foster**, Produced by **Hal Roach**, Edited by **Richard Currier**, Filmed - Mar/Apr 1929, Released - May 4, 1929 by MGM, Running time - 2 reels.

With: **Mae Busch** (Mrs Barbara Hardy), **Thelma Todd** (Mrs Kennedy), **Edgar Kennedy** (Officer Kennedy).

"The world over - a wife loves to have her husband bring a friend home to dinner - as a surprise."

Ollie has promised Stan a home cooked slap-up meal. Mrs Hardy however has other ideas and fed up with cooking for all her husband's friends, leaves home. Ollie tries to cook dinner himself, but has trouble lighting the gas stove and is blown through the door as a result. Mrs Kennedy, a pretty blonde across the hall, hears the commotion and offers to cook the meal. She too has difficulty with the stove and emerges from the kitchen with her dress smouldering. She is about to go and change, when she spots her husband returning home from work. As Officer Kennedy is an extremely jealous husband she stays put in the Hardy apartment. Things become complicated when Mrs Hardy also returns, so Mrs Kennedy hides in a trunk. Realising the predicament he is now in, Ollie tells his wife all is over between them and with trunk packed is leaving for South America that very night. Stan is branded a home wrecker as Mrs Hardy hurls crockery around the room. Officer Kennedy investigates and soon finds out the boys are up to no good. He tells Ollie's wife to make the boys a nice meal while he takes them into the hall to give them a good talking to. Wanting a piece of the action himself, Kennedy tells the boys to take the trunk into his apartment where he confesses about his own womanising while out on the beat, ignorant of the fact that his wife is listening to his bragging from inside the trunk. The boys nervously sit down to their meal, more concerned about the goings-on across the hall. All hell breaks loose in the Kennedy apartment and Mr. Kennedy interrupts the meal sporting a black eye. Ollie is summoned to the hall, returning seconds later with a bruised nose. Next it's Stan's turn, and he's about to get the same treatment when Mrs Kennedy smashes a large

What Was The Film When..?

vase over her husband's head, knocking him cold. Stan re-enters the Hardy apartment and bids his farewell to Ollie, who is astonished to see Kennedy in a crumpled heap on the floor. Stan swaggers his way down the hall before coming a cropper as he falls head first down the stairs.

'Now I'll tell ya, we're gonna have meat, we're gonna have a great big juicy steak...' The first audible words (spoken by Ollie) heard in Laurel and Hardy's debut talking picture. Ollie's extravagant description of the lavish meal, followed by Stan's simple and amusing reply of *'Any nuts?'* was the boys' first verbal exchange. Ollie was also to utter *'Why don't you do something to help me'* in this film, a trademark cry for help, which would be repeated many times in future films. The death knell had sounded for many silent movie stars, when in October 1927, Al Jolson appeared in the talking picture, the Warner Brothers' produced THE JAZZ SINGER (Charlie Chaplin did not release his first talking picture, THE GREAT DICTATOR, until 1940). Not so for Laurel and Hardy whose voices perfectly matched the characters they had portrayed in their silent days. Appropriately titled, the film marked the debut with the boys of Thelma Todd (born Lawrence Mass. 1905) who would later co-star in her own Roach series with ZaSu Pitts and then Patsy Kelly. Such was the urgency to release a "talkie," UNACCUSTOMED AS WE ARE was released on May 4, 1929, before the boys' final three silents DOUBLE WHOOPEE, BACON GRABBERS and ANGORA LOVE.

BERTH MARKS

Directed by **Lewis Foster**, Produced by **Hal Roach**, Edited by **Richard Currier**, Filmed - Apr 1929, Released - Jun 1, 1929 by MGM, Running time - 2 reels.

With: **Pat Harmon** (Station announcer), **Silas Wilcox** (Conductor), **Charlie Hall, Paulette Goddard, Harry Bernard, Baldwin Cooke** (Train passengers).

"Mr. Hardy told Mr. Laurel to meet him at the Santa Fe Station at a quarter of ten - but Mr. Laurel became confused, and thought he meant 9:45."

Did You Know Laughing Gravy had quite an illustrious movie career. Apart from roles in Laurel and Hardy films, the little dog appeared in ten other pictures.

Any Nuts?

Ollie is the manager and Stan the fiddle player in what they think is a big time vaudeville act. They meet up at the railway station to catch an overnight train to Pottsville where they have an engagement. They nearly miss the train when they have trouble understanding the incoherent station announcer, and then leave their music strewn all over the platform and track. On board, Stan upsets a lady passenger when he walks into her berth while she is undressing. He beats a hasty retreat while the lady's husband (Charlie Hall) mistakes an innocent bystander (Harry Bernard) as the intruder and rips his jacket in half. He in turn attacks another passenger and repeats the jacket-ripping episode, and before long a clothes-tearing episode has broken out. In the sleeping carriage, Stan and Ollie attempt to climb into their cramped top berth, disturbing other passengers with their efforts. Meanwhile, the clothes ripping has reached epidemic proportions with the whole train now seemingly involved. Eventually after much huffing and puffing, the boys manage to change into their night-shirts, and are just about to settle down for the night, when the conductor announces the next stop...Pottsville! They hurriedly gather their clothes and get off the train. As it pulls away, they start to dress on the track side before Ollie realises Stan has left the fiddle on the train, so chases him down the track.

Charlie Chaplin's future wife, Paulette Goddard, plays a small part in this film as a train passenger. Improvisation by Stan and Ollie on set would become the norm in Laurel and Hardy films, with the boys openly ad-libbing as they went along. This was evident in the hilarious upper berth scene, which dominates the film. It would be re-worked (to lesser effect) in their 1944 20th Century-Fox picture THE BIG NOISE.

MEN O' WAR

Directed by **Lewis Foster**, Produced by **Hal Roach**, Edited by **Richard Currier**, Filmed - May 1929, Released - Jun 29, 1929 by MGM, Running time - 2 reels.

With: **James Finlayson** (Park/Soda attendant), **Anne Cornwall** (Stan's date who loves soldiers), **Gloria Greer** (Ollie's date), **Harry Bernard** (Policeman), **Charlie Hall**, **Baldwin Cooke** (Battling boaters), **Peter Gordon** (Bicycle rider who falls in the lake).

(Waiter) 'What would you have sir?' (Stan) 'I think I'll try some of that demitasse.' (Waiter) 'Yes sir.'
(Stan) 'And bring me a cup of coffee too.' (*SWISS MISS*)

What Was The Film When..?

On shore leave from the navy, Stan and Ollie are strolling through the park where they find a pair of lady's bloomers (dropped earlier from a laundry basket). When they notice two girlfriends searching for something, they put two and two together, and as usual make five. One of the ladies describes her lost article as '*white and easy to pull on*,' and the boys are just about to hand over their find when a policeman intervenes, handing over a pair of white gloves to the grateful lady. After the slight misunderstanding, Ollie bashfully asks the girls to accompany them to the soda fountain. One of the girls comments how much she likes "soldiers" so Ollie introduces her to Stan "the general." At the soda fountain the boys realise their bank roll only amounts to 15 cents, so to save face, Ollie tells Stan to refuse a drink when asked. Unable to grasp the severity of their financial situation, Stan drinks all of Ollie's soda, which they were to share, so is given the bill that amounts to 30 cents. Left with no alternative, Stan gambles their total assets on the fruit machine and wins the jackpot. With their new found wealth, the foursome hire a rowing boat with Stan taking up the oars. Regrettably his navy training didn't seem to include the art of rowing, and despite his best efforts the boat keeps going round in circles. Ollie's attempts are no better and they collide with another boater (Charlie Hall). A pillow fight ensues before Stan pushes their rival into the lake. Wet and bedraggled, he climbs back aboard, as other boats collide and capsize. More and more boaters swim to the boys' vessel to join the free-for-all. The park attendant and a policeman try to row out to the disturbance, but they also overturn and have to swim over to the warring parties. When they try to climb aboard the already overcrowded boat, it proves too much and it starts to sink, with the battle still going strong.

The soda fountain sketch was an improved interpretation of the original used in the 1928 silent SHOULD MARRIED MEN GO HOME?

THE HOLLYWOOD REVUE OF 1929*

Directed by **Charles Riesner**, Produced by **Harry Rapf**, Edited by **William Gray & Cameron Wood**, Filmed - Jun 1929, Released - Nov 23, 1929 by MGM, Running time - 120 minutes.

With: **Jack Benny & Conrad Nagel** (as the Masters of Ceremonies), **Stan Laurel, Oliver Hardy, Joan Crawford, John Gilbert, Norma Shearer, Bessie Love, Buster Keaton, William Haines, Owen Lee, Marie Dressler, Polly Moran, Marion Davies, Gus Edwards, Lionel

Any Nuts?

Barrymore, Anita Page, Nils Asther, The Brox Sisters, Charles King, Dane and Arthur, Albertina Rasch Ballet, Cliff "Ukelele Ike" Edwards.

Compere Jack Benny is about to introduce the next act on the bill, when the curtains open to reveal the boys preparing and rehearsing their magic act, with Ollie busy hiding the props in Stan's overcoat, unaware that the compere is watching. Ollie reminds Stan not to tip his hat, before being alerted to the fact that the curtains are open. He introduces himself to the compere with a tip of his hat. Stan, forgetting his instructions, does the same, and the first trick of the act is ruined, when a concealed dove flies away. The boys fall out over the ruined trick, and a pinching pushing, stamping match develops, until Ollie puts his hand into a bowl of eggs, thus ruining another part of the show. The bowl of smashed eggs is tossed into the wings, narrowly missing the compere. Ollie finally begins the act by changing a candle into a vase of flowers, the illusion performed behind a large black cloth held by Stan, who then ruins the trick when he picks up both the candle and the flowers in full view of the audience. Undeterred by their failures, Ollie announces the big finale. Stan hands him a large cream cake, but Ollie slips on a banana skin left from a previously failed trick, and dives head first into it. Ollie throws the remnants into the wings, with compere Jack Benny returning to the stage seconds later covered in it. Seemingly unconcerned by it all, Mr. Benny introduces the next act on the bill.
(*Stan and Ollie part only)

Now that the silent era was all but dead, the major studios were keen to show off their stars, with MGM's bash running for a whopping two hours. Included in the revue were John Gilbert and Norma Shearer bringing the balcony scene from Romeo and Juliet up to date, while Buster Keaton cavorted around stage as an Egyptian dancer. Stan and Ollie were added to the cast to add some comedy relief to the show. Despite poor reviews THE HOLLYWOOD REVUE OF 1929 was nominated for the 1928-29 Oscars for best picture.

PERFECT DAY

Directed by **James Parrott**, Produced by **Hal Roach**, Edited by **Richard Currier**, Filmed - Jun 1929, Released - Aug 10, 1929 by MGM, Running time - 2 reels.

(Stan) 'He fell through a trapdoor and broke his neck.' (Ollie) 'Was he building a house?'
(Stan) 'No they were hanging him.' *(THE LAUREL – HARDY MURDER CASE)*

What Was The Film When..?

With: **Edgar Kennedy** (Uncle Edgar), **Kay Deslys** (Mrs Hardy), **Isabelle Keith** (Mrs Laurel), **Baldwin Cooke, Lyle Tayo** (Next door neighbours), **Clara Guiol, Harry Bernard** (Neighbours across the road), **Charley Rogers** (Parson).

Also appeared: Buddy the dog.

The Laurels and the Hardys, along with their gout-ridden Uncle Edgar, plan a Sunday trip into the country for a picnic. The boys are given the job of preparing the sandwiches, but when Stan knocks the heavily laden tray out of Ollie's grasp, a fight breaks out, with sandwiches thrown all over the room. The wives act as peacemakers and the boys soon make up. With everything prepared they clamber aboard the car, bidding farewell to the neighbours. The journey is temporarily halted when the car develops a flat tyre. The boys set about changing it, with Stan causing untold misery for Uncle Edgar when he steps on his aching foot, and then traps it in the car door. They change the tyre, only to put the punctured one back on. When Ollie realises the mistake, he hurls the tyre jack at Stan, but misses and smashes the window of the next door neighbour, who promptly returns it via the car windscreen. Just as the situation begins to get out of hand, the local parson walks down the street and everyone heads indoors. Again they climb aboard the car, and once again say their goodbyes to the neighbours, but this time the car refuses to start. Ollie asks Stan to help him by "throwing out the clutch," which he does literally, ripping it from it's housing and flinging it onto the road. Miraculously the car starts, and after saying their farewells, they drive into a road under repair, sinking without trace into a large water-filled hole.

Stan Laurel and the writers were never afraid to repeat a comedy situation. The ending to the film was a virtual repeat of the final moments in LEAVE 'EM LAUGHING, done just eighteen months previous.

THEY GO BOOM

Directed by **James Parrott**, Produced by **Hal Roach**, Edited by **Richard Currier**, Filmed - Jul 1929, Released - Sep 21, 1929 by MGM, Running time - 2 reels.

With: **Charlie Hall** (Landlord), **Sam Lufkin** (Policeman).

84   (Ollie) 'Agnes, meet your new master, Lord Flagpole Crabtree.' *(ANOTHER FINE MESS)*

Any Nuts?

"3 A.M. - Mr. Hardy had the sniffles - His carburetor hadn't been right for days and days."

It's the middle of the night and the boys' attempts at sleep are hindered by Ollie's sneezing, due to a heavy cold. Matters are not helped when Ollie is drenched after Stan punctures a water pipe whilst attempting to re-hang a picture displaced during one of Ollie's sneezing bouts. With Ollie liable to die of "ammonia," Stan prepares him a mustard foot bath. Ollie complains that the water is too hot, so Stan fetches a bucket of cold water, but slips and again soaks his roommate through. Fed up with Stan's incompetence, one thing leads to another and the pair become involved in a pushing match. During this the bed's air mattress gets punctured, so Ollie re-inflates it using the gas pipe hose in their room. The landlord investigates the noise and ends up wearing the contents of the footbath before storming out, promising to get even. The boys try to get some sleep, but as Ollie climbs into bed, his dressing gown snags the gas tap, causing the mattress to further inflate and rise slowly to the ceiling. They realise their predicament when Stan bangs his head on the ceiling, as the landlord bursts into the room with a policeman. With the mattress on the verge of exploding, the landlord and cop beat a hasty retreat, while Ollie again develops the sniffles. Despite Stan's pleas not to sneeze, he does just that and the mattress blows up, totally wrecking the bedsit. The landlord returns with reinforcements just as another sneeze brings down the ceiling, covering them all in debris.

THE HOOSE-GOW

Directed by **James Parrott**, Produced by **Hal Roach**, Edited by **Richard Currier**, Filmed - Aug/Sep 1929, Released - Nov 16, 1929 by MGM, Running time - 2 reels.

With: **Tiny Sandford** (Prison guard, Sandford), **James Finlayson** (Prison governor), **Leo Willis** (Lag planning breakout), **Ellinor Vanderveer** (Governer's guest), **Dick Sutherland** (Prison cook), **Charlie Hall** (Guard in lookout post), **Sam Lufkin** (Prison camp officer).

Also appeared: Retta Palmer, Eddie Dunn, Baldwin Cooke, Jack Ward, Ham Kinsey, John Whiteford, Ed Brandenberg, Chet Brandenberg, Charles Dorety.

What Was The Film When..?

"Neither Mr. Laurel nor Mr. Hardy had any thoughts of doing wrong. As a matter of fact, they had no thoughts of any kind."

The boys are on the way to prison, despite their protestations that they were only watching the raid. On arrival, they are ordered to stand by the wall, but Ollie's pre-arranged breakout with another prisoner (Leo Willis) is foiled when a burly guard (Tiny Sandford) chases off the would-be-rescuers, after seeing a rope ladder appear from over the wall. Set to work digging ditches spells big trouble for Ollie, who has his hat speared and coat ripped by his pick-wielding friend. The dinner bell sounds and the boys arrive at the mess table only to find there are no seats left. They are directed to a table that actually belongs to the burly guard who is away answering a telephone call. Ollie finds out the truth when he pours his soup over the guard's foot as he returns to the table. Ordered away and still hungry, they head for the cook's tent where they are told to chop wood if they want to eat - the more they chop, the more they can eat. With this in mind Ollie chops down a tree not realising that it's actually a lookout post, which crashes down, guard and all, demolishing the mess tent. Later that day the prison governor arrives with other dignitaries to inspect the prisoners working. Stan and Ollie are back digging ditches, where Stan's pick becomes tangled in Ollie's uniform. Ollie rips the pick free and hurls it away - looking on in horror as it embeds itself in the radiator of the governor's car causing it to spurt water. Another jailbird suggests they fill the radiator with rice to stem the flow, and sure enough the remedy works, until the car is started up and rice spews out to form a pool of gunge on the floor. Stan and Ollie are asked if they are responsible, but when Stan acts dumb to the question, he is kicked head first into the mess by the guard. Stan picks up a handful of the rice and shoves it into the face of the guard, who responds by hurling a handful back, only to splat the governor instead. It isn't long before a rice throwing brawl breaks out with prisoners, guards and dignitaries all involved. During the mayhem, the boys seize the opportunity to try and escape by hiding in the back of one of the cars. However, their jailbreak is soon over when the car reverses into a paint truck and two large barrels of whitewash spill into the back of the vehicle, covering them from head to toe.

86   (Ollie's wife) 'What are you doing?' (Stan) 'I'm making myself a malted milk.' (Ollie's wife) 'Oh...how long does it take?' (Stan) 'About fifteen minutes to a quarter of an hour.' *(THE BOHEMIAN GIRL)*

Any Nuts?

THE ROGUE SONG

Directed by **Lionel Barrymore**, Produced by **Irving Thalberg***, Edited by **Margaret Booth**, Filmed - Jul-Sep 1929, Released - May 10, 1930 by MGM, Running time - 115 minutes.
*not credited

With: **Lawrence Tibbett** (Yegor), **Oliver Hardy** (Murza-Bek), **Stan Laurel** (Ali-Bek), **Catherine Dale Owen** (Princess Vera), **Judith Voselli** (Countess Tatiana), **Ulrich Haupt** (Prince Sergei), **Florence Lake** (Nadja), **Nance O'Neil** (Princess Alexandra), **Lionel Belmore** (Ossman), **Kate Price** (Petrovina), **Wallace McDonald** (Hassan), **Burr McIntosh** (Count Peter).

Also appeared: James Bradbury Jnr., Elsa Alsen, H. A. Morgan, Harry Bernard, The Albertina Rasch Ballet.

Stan and Ollie are side-kicks to Yegor, a Russian bandit nicknamed "The Singing Bandit of Agrakhan" who falls in love with Princess Vera. This leads to complications as her brother Prince Sergei commands a Cossack army who are his deadly enemies.

Based on *Gypsy Love*, an operetta written in 1910 by Franz Lehar. THE ROGUE SONG was intended to show off the singing talents of baritone Lawrence Tibbett, in this, his debut film. Stan and Ollie were added to the cast with production near to completion, to give the film some comic relief. The picture was shot in two colour Technicolor, but despite an extensive search, only some negatives of the film have so far been located, after the original print was destroyed by fire in the MGM storage vaults (the soundtrack disc survived). Fortunately Stan and Ollie appear in the majority of a clip that exists. They take shelter in a dark cave on a stormy night after their tent blows away. Ollie asks Stan if he is wearing a fur coat, only realising his mistake, when out of the darkness echoes the growl of a ferocious bear. Lawrence Tibbett's performance warranted a 1929-30 Oscar nomination for best actor.

(Lola Marcel) 'Tell me about my dear dear daddy, is it true that's he's dead?'
(Stan) 'Well we hope he is, they buried him.' *(WAY OUT WEST)*

What Was The Film When..?

NIGHT OWLS

Directed by **James Parrott**, Produced by **Hal Roach**, Edited by **Richard Currier**, Filmed - Oct/Nov 1929, Released - Jan 4, 1930 by MGM, Running time - 2 reels.

With: **Edgar Kennedy** (Officer Kennedy), **Anders Randolph** (Chief of police), **James Finlayson** (Meadows the butler), **Harry Bernard** (Desk sergeant), **Charles McMurphy**, **Baldwin Cooke** (Officers).

Officer Kennedy is in the mire with his police chief, after a spate of forty-two burglaries in just one week, all of which go unpunished due to Kennedy's non-existent arrest rate. The chief warns him that if any more burglaries occur without arrests, he will be fired. This causes great amusement among the other officers, who comment that the only way Kennedy would apprehend anybody is to set up the robbery himself. That night on patrol, Kennedy finds Stan and Ollie asleep on a park bench and threatens them with ninety days on the rock pile, unless they help him to get on the right side of the chief. He tells the boys of his plan, for them to rob the chief's house, with himself arriving just in the nick of time to make the arrest. Left with no alternative, the boys are led to the back of the chief's house, where they scale the wall and crash down through a glass lean-to. This alerts the butler of the house who blames the noise on cats. The boys start to meow loudly and are hit by shoes thrown by the butler from an upstairs window. Stan is about to throw a house brick back, but Ollie lobs it over the wall and unwittingly knocks Kennedy out, waiting on the other side. After several attempts to gain entry into the house through the front door and window, they finally break in and start to fill their swag bag. While they sit down to wait for Kennedy's grand entrance, Ollie accidentally turns on the automatic piano. The music alerts the chief, who armed with his gun, heads downstairs to investigate. Meanwhile Kennedy has recovered and with all guns blazing, makes a dramatic entry. This scares the boys so much, they climb out of the window, just as the chief switches on the light to find Kennedy standing in the middle of the room clutching the swag bag. He is blamed for all the recent robberies and promised a life sentence, while for once, Stan and Ollie get away scot-free.

(Alf Laurel) 'You're sure looking good Stanley, but how you've altered.'
(Stan) 'You've altered too, but you haven't changed a bit...has he Ollie?' (OUR RELATIONS)

Any Nuts?

To maintain the boys' ever-growing popularity in Europe, NIGHT OWLS became the first multi-language release, with Stan and Ollie speaking their lines in the appropriate language, with the help of interpreters and idiot boards. This development allowed foreign audiences to hear Laurel and Hardy's own voices for the first time. The Spanish version was entitled LADRONES and the Italian LADRONI, both running for four reels.

BLOTTO

Directed by **James Parrott**, Produced by **Hal Roach**, Edited by **Richard Currier**, Filmed - Dec 1929, Released - Feb 8, 1930 by MGM, Running time - 3 reels.

With: **Anita Garvin** (Mrs Laurel), **Tiny Sandford**, **Baldwin Cooke** (Waiters), **Frank Holliday** (Cabaret singer), **Charlie Hall** (Cab driver).

Also appeared: Dick Gilbert, Jack Hill.

Stan is meeting Ollie for a night out on the town but can't think of a suitable excuse to get out of the house and away from his high and mighty wife. Ollie phones Stan telling him that he's booked a table at the newly opened Rainbow Club, and comes up with an idea for Stan to send himself a telegram calling him out on urgent business. Thinking this a good idea, Stan promises to bring along a bottle of liquor that Mrs Laurel has been saving since prohibition, blaming the theft on the ice man. Unfortunately for Stan, his wife has been listening to their conversation on the upstairs telephone and decides to scupper their plans. She creeps downstairs, drains the bottle and re-fills it with cold tea, pepper, mustard and other foul-tasting ingredients. The boys arrive at the club and it isn't long before they uncork the bottle and drink what they think is good tasting "liquor." They soon begin to act very drunk, and before long are in fits of laughter. Their fun is cut short however when Mrs Laurel enters the club and informs them that they have only been drinking cold tea. The boys soon sober up when she unwraps a shotgun and chases them out of the club, firing at them as they jump into a cab, blowing it to pieces.

Did You Know Charlie Hall stood only 5' 3" tall, Daphne Pollard 4' 9"!

What Was The Film When..?

A storyline that overran usually ended up on the editor's floor. The material written for BLOTTO warranted it becoming Stan and Ollie's first regular three-reel picture. It was re-filmed in Spanish as LA VIDA NOCTURNA (with Linda Loredo as Mrs Laurel) and French as UNE NUIT EXTRAVAGANTE (Georgette Rhodes playing Stan's wife), with both films running for four reels. BLOTTO contained one of Laurel and Hardy's best and most loved sketches. Stan, seemingly the worse for wear after draining the bottle he has stolen from his wife, is moved to tears with the club singer's rendition of 'The Curse Of An Aching Heart.' Within seconds though, Stan's emotions turn full circle and his giggle turns to side-splitting laughter. The laughter scene proved infectious to cinema audiences as well. It was repeated with similar effect in SCRAM! (1932) and again in FRA DIAVOLO (1933). Frivolity was also common on the set with practical jokes and general tomfoolery helping create the family atmosphere the studios were so famed for. Supporting cast usually appeared in the films using their own christian or surnames, and in BLOTTO, Ollie even quotes Stan's real home telephone number of the time - Oxford 0614!!!

BRATS

Directed by **James Parrott**, Produced by **Hal Roach**, Edited by **Richard Currier**, Filmed - Jan 1930, Released - Mar 22, 1930 by MGM, Running time - 2 reels.

With: **Stan Laurel and Oliver Hardy** also playing their sons, Stanley and Oliver (Jean Harlow in photograph only).

"Mr. Laurel and Mr. Hardy remained at home to take care of the children - Their wives had gone out to target practice."

Stan and Ollie's attempts at recreation are constantly hindered by the antics of their young sons Stanley and Oliver. When a vase is broken, the youngsters are ordered to bed where the squabble is continued. Ollie threatens to breaks both their necks, until Stan reminds him of the old adage *'You can lead a horse to water, but a pencil must be lead.'* With this Ollie offers a nickel to the first one undressed and into bed, a contest that Stanley easily wins, until his

(Ollie) 'Well if you must know, were going to humiliate ourselves by begging for food.'
(Stan) 'What again?' *(ONE GOOD TURN)*

Any Nuts ?

Anita Garvin
1907? - 1994

playmate notices that he still has his clothes on underneath his night shirt. Oliver claims the money for himself and puts it in his mouth for safe keeping, so Stanley punches him in the stomach and it is swallowed. They then spot a mouse in the bedroom and try to catch it. Stanley fires at the mouse with his popgun but hits Oliver on the backside. Stanley fills the bath so that Oliver can bathe the wound whilst balanced precariously on a stool at the bath's edge. Stanley then accidentally knocks the stool, sending his playmate toppling into the water. As he tries to climb out of the bath, he inadvertently switches on the shower causing the bath to overflow and start to flood the bathroom. Oliver slips on the wet floor, sending plaster crashing down on their fathers playing pool in the room below. The parents rush upstairs and try and get their boys to sleep with Ollie singing them a lullaby, which seems to do the trick, until Stan joins in and immediately wakes them. The children promise to go to sleep if they can have a glass of water, so Stan starts towards the bathroom but is stopped by Ollie who is worried that he might spill the drinks. Ollie opens the bathroom door to be met by a torrent of water that sweeps him and Stan off their feet, flooding the bedroom.

BRATS became the first regular film to use 'The Cuckoo Song' (or 'Ku-Ku Song') to accompany the opening titles, although sources suggest NIGHT OWLS was the first to use the tune. The ditty, originally written as an hourly time signal on the KFVD radio station situated on the Roach Studios site, was to become Stan and Ollie's instantly recognisable signature tune. It was written by Marvin Hatley, who was Musical Director for the Roach Studios in the late 1930's, receiving three Oscar nominations for his work. Hatley along with Leroy Shield would be responsible for the majority of the catchy tunes heard in the boys' films. The German version of BRATS released was titled GLUCKLICHE KINDHEIT.

BELOW ZERO

Directed by **James Parrott**, Produced by **Hal Roach**, Edited by **Richard Currier**, Filmed - Feb/Mar 1930, Released - Apr 26, 1930 by MGM, Running time - 2 reels.

With: **Frank Holliday** (Policeman), **Tiny Sandford** (Pete, owner of diner), **Charlie Hall** (Street cleaner), **Leo Willis** (Chasing ruffian),

Any Nuts?

Bobby Burns (Blind man), **Kay Deslys** (Lady at upstairs window), **Baldwin Cooke** (Man at upstairs window), **Blanche Payson** (Tough lady).

Also appeared: Lyle Tayo, Retta Palmer, Jack Hill, Charley Sullivan, Charles McMurphy, Bob O'Conor.

"The freezing winter of '29 will long be remembered - Mr. Hardy's nose was so blue, Mr. Laurel shot it for a jay-bird."

The boys are trying to scrape a living as street musicians in the bleak winter of 1929. Their cause isn't helped when they sing *In The Good Old Summertime* during a snow storm, and then realise they have been playing outside a deaf and dumb institute! Setting up outside a Chinese restaurant, a lady (Kay Deslys) hears their performance and asks how much they earn per street. When Ollie tells her 50 cents, she tosses them a dollar and asks them to move down a couple of streets! Their playing then upsets a street cleaner and a snowball fight ensues. When a tough looking lady (Blanche Payson) also becomes implicated, she smashes Ollie's double bass over his head and throws Stan's harmonium into the street where it is flattened by a truck. The boys luck seems to change when Stan spots a well-laden wallet lying in the snow. A ruffian witnesses their good fortune and follows, before a policeman intervenes. To show their appreciation they invite the cop for a slap up meal, and three 'T' bone steaks are soon devoured. When it is time to pay the bill, the boys discover the wallet actually belongs to the policeman, who accuses them of being pick-pockets. The cop pays his part of the bill, and instead of arresting the boys, leaves them to the mercy of the burly owner and his heavies. Ollie is thrown into the street but is unable to find Stan, until he hears a gurgling sound coming from a rain barrel. Stan emerges with a huge bloated stomach, having drunk all the water inside.

The three-reel Spanish version was entitled TIEMBLA Y TITUBEA.

HOG WILD

Directed by **James Parrott**, Produced by **Hal Roach**, Edited by **Richard Currier**, Filmed - Apr 1930, Released - May 31, 1930 by MGM, Running time - 2 reels.

With: **Fay Holderness** (Mrs Hardy), **Dorothy Granger** (Tillie the maid/Lady by puddle), **Charles McMurphy** (Streetcar conductor).

What Was The Film When..?

"Amnesia! Mr. Hardy was beginning to forget things, but Mr. Laurel had no fear of losing his memory - As a matter of fact, Mr. Laurel never had a memory to lose."

Ollie has an appointment with Stan. However, before he can go anywhere his wife insists he puts up an aerial on the roof, as the radio hasn't worked for the last three months. Stan arrives and agrees to help complete the simple task. Several broken windows later the boys climb onto the roof, with Ollie soon back on terra-firma when he slips on the aerial pole and dives head first into the fish pond. Back on the roof, Ollie decides to play safe by fastening a rope around his waist, with the other end tied around the chimney stack. With Stan on his back, Ollie then slips on a loose tile, and both fall into the fish pond, closely followed by the chimney. Determined to finish the job, and with the ladder positioned on the back of Stan's car, Ollie is half way up, when Stan accidentally starts the vehicle. It speeds through the streets, with Ollie balanced precariously on the ladder. After several near misses he finally comes to grief, falling flat on his face. Mrs Hardy arrives on the scene in tears, and thinking she is upset over his dice with death, Ollie tries to comfort her, only to be told that the radio has been taken away by the finance company. To make matters worse, Stan's car refuses to start and is hit by a tram.

Foreign releases of HOG WILD included the French PELE MELE, and the Spanish RADIO-MANIA (with Yola D'Avril as Mrs Hardy). In Britain it was released under the title AERIAL ANTICS.

THE LAUREL-HARDY MURDER CASE

Directed by **James Parrott**, Produced by **Hal Roach**, Edited by **Richard Currier**, Filmed - May 1930, Released - Sep 6, 1930 by MGM, Running time - 3 reels.

With: **Del Henderson** (Disguised housekeeper), **Fred Kelsey** (Police chief), **Tiny Sandford** (Policeman), **Bobby Burns** (Nervous relative), **Art Rowlands** (Relative with theatre tickets), **Dorothy Granger** (Relative), **Stanley Blystone** (Detective), **Frank Austin** (Butler), **Lon Poff, Rosa Gore** (Elderly couple).

"Mr. Laurel and Mr. Hardy decided that they needed a rest - They had been looking for work since 1921."

(Stan) 'What's the matter?' (Ollie) 'Didn't you read it?'
(Stan) 'Yeh, but I wasn't listening.' *(BEAU HUNKS)*

Any Nuts?

Out of work again, the boys are on the quayside, with Stan fishing for his supper as Ollie tries to sleep. Ollie wakes and reads an article in a newspaper about the wealthy Ebeneezer Laurel who has passed away leaving a $3 million estate. With the legal heirs being sought for the reading of the will at eight o'clock that evening, Ollie asks Stan if he had such a relative. Stan tells him a story about an uncle who had fallen through a trapdoor and broken his neck - when they were hanging him! They arrive at the Laurel mansion during a storm, with Ollie hoping to persuade everyone that Stan is the rightful heir. They are informed that they have to spend the night in the house as the police chief suspects that one of the relatives present is guilty of foul play and that Ebeneezer was actually murdered. The boys are shown to their room, which happens to be the very one where Ebeneezer was found dead. During the night the relatives, one by one, disappear after receiving a mysterious phone call. The boys receive a fright when the lamp stand appears to "chase" them down the stairs, and another scare when a bat flies under the bedclothes. With all the relatives out of the way, Stan is called to the phone by the butler and the housekeeper, who is in drag and stands to inherit the estate if there are no relatives left. Ollie is about to be stabbed by the housekeeper, but Stan saves his pal by slugging the villain. A fierce struggle follows, when suddenly the boys are wrestling each other back on the quayside, before rolling off and into the water. It has all been just a bad dream!!

Extended German (**DER SPUK UM MITTERNACHT**), Spanish (**NOCHE DE DUENDES**) and French (**FEU MON ONCLE**) versions were also produced, each incorporating excerpts from **BERTH MARKS**.

PARDON US

Directed by **James Parrott**, Produced by **Hal Roach**, Edited by **Richard Currier**, Filmed - Jun-Nov 1930, Released - Aug 15, 1931 by MGM, Running time - 56 minutes.

With: **Walter Long** ("The Tiger"), **Wilfred Lucas** (Warden), **James Finlayson** (Prison schoolteacher), **Otto Fries** (Dentist), **Charlie Hall** (Dental assistant), **Tiny Sandford** (Prison guard, Shields), **Sam Lufkin** (Guard), **Harry Bernard** (Desk sergeant, Warren), **June Marlowe** (Warden's daughter), **Leo Willis** (Cohort of "The Tiger"), **Frank Holliday** (Guard in school room), **Bobby Burns** (Patient at dentist's), **Eddie Baker** (Overseer at cotton fields).

(Ollie) 'What are you eating?' (Stan) 'An apple.' (Ollie) 'Where d'ya get it?' (Stan) 'In there.'
(Ollie) 'Why that's not real fruit, it's imitation, it's made of wax!' (SONS OF THE DESERT)

What Was The Film When..?

Walter Long
1879 - 1952

Any Nuts?

Also appeared: Frank Austin, Robert Kortman, Jerry Mandy, Bobby Dunn, Eddie Dunn, Baldwin Cooke, Charles Dorety, Dick Gilbert, Will Stanton, Jack Hill, Gene Morgan, Charles Bachman, Charley Rogers, Gordon Douglas, Silas Wilcox, James Parrott, Hal Roach, The Etude Ethiopian Chorus, Belle the bloodhound.

> *"Mr. Hardy is a man of wonderful ideas - So is Mr. Laurel - as long as he doesn't try to think."*

The boys are small time beer brewers during the prohibition. Unfortunately Stan tries to sell some to a policeman, mistaking him for a street car conductor, and the boys end up in prison. Stan is soon making enemies inside when his loose tooth, which makes a "raspberry blowing" sound every time he speaks, upsets the guards and the warden. They are put in a cell with "The Tiger," the prison's toughest inmate, who befriends Stan, thinking that any man who dares to blow raspberries at him must be a brave man indeed. After a spell in solitary confinement for ruining the prison school teacher's lesson, Stan and Ollie become innocently involved in "The Tiger's" jailbreak, and end up the only ones not recaptured. A $500 reward is posted as they take refuge in a Negro community by blacking their faces and working in the cotton fields, even making the prison bloodhounds their pets. One particular day, the warden's car grinds to a halt right next to the field where they are working. Stan and Ollie offer their assistance, safe in the knowledge that their disguise won't give them away. The fault is soon rectified as the car has only run out of petrol, and the warden is just about to drive off when Stan bids him goodbye, only for his loose tooth to give him away and blow their disguises. After another lengthy spell in solitary, Stan is sent to the dentist to have the tooth pulled, but is reluctant to have treatment after seeing a fellow patient wheeled out on a stretcher. Ollie takes the chair and is showing Stan how to relax, when the dentist comes up behind him and extracts one of his teeth instead. "The Tiger" meanwhile has planned another bust out, but this time the warden is wise to it after one of the guards overhears Stan and Ollie talking about it in the yard. In the dining room the weapons to be used for the breakout are distributed under the table, but when Stan is handed a machine gun it goes off. The prisoners try to fight their way out, with the uprising soon quelled by the guards and the army. The boys are deemed heroes by the warden, who thinks Stan's firing of the machine gun was intended as a warning. They are both handed a pardon and told to start life again where they left off. Stan takes him for his word and is immediately back in the doghouse when he tries to sell the warden a couple of cases of beer!

Even though Stan and Ollie's popularity was at an all time high, the move into feature films was still considered a big gamble, with the boys unsure themselves whether they could make the transition to pictures lasting three times as long as the conventional two-reeler. PARDON US, a parody of MGM's 1930 film THE BIG HOUSE did in fact start out as a short, and was extended to feature length to justify the cost of the expensive set built for the prison scenes. Their initial fears about the switch to features were soon dispelled as it proved a box-office smash. It incorporated the dentist sketch from LEAVE 'EM LAUGHING, with Otto Fries again wrongly extracting one of Ollie's teeth. Hal Roach and James Parrott also figured in the film, and can be seen marching in formation with the other prisoners shortly after the boys' second spell in solitary (Hal Roach is directly in front of Ollie, with James Parrott on Ollie's right). The foreign versions included the French SOUS LES VERROUS featuring Boris Karloff, the German HINTER SCHLOSS UND RIEGEL, the Italian MURAGLIE and the Spanish DE BOTE EN BOTE. In Britain it was released under the title JAILBIRDS.

ANOTHER FINE MESS

Directed by **James Parrott**, Produced by **Hal Roach**, Edited by **Richard Currier**, Filmed - Sep/Oct 1930, Released - Nov 29, 1930 by MGM, Running time - 3 reels.

With: **James Finlayson** (Colonel Buckshot), **Charles Gerrard** (Lord Leopold/Ambrose Plumtree), **Thelma Todd** (Lady Plumtree), **Harry Bernard** (Policeman), **Eddie Dunn** (Meadows the butler), **Gertrude Sutton** (Maid), **Bobby Burns** (Bicycle rider), **Bill Knight**, **Bob Mimford** (Officers), **Joe Mole** (Half of gnu on bike).

> "Mr. Laurel and Mr. Hardy have many ups and downs -
> Mr. Hardy takes charge of the upping, and Mr. Laurel
> does most of the downing."

(Stan) 'But suppose we meet this Diavolo?' (Ollie) 'All we have to do is watch our P's and Q's – don't you think that I know a bandit when I see one?' (Stan) 'Well I don't want to walk around with my throat cut.' *(FRA DIAVOLO)*

Any Nuts ?

A policeman is chasing the boys down the street having found them asleep on a park bench. They hide in the basement of a large mansion belonging to a Colonel Wilburforce Buckshot, who has advertised the house for rent, after leaving for a hunting trip to South Africa. The butler and maid of the house also decide to go on vacation, taking full advantage of their master's absence. The boys are about to leave, when a Lord and Lady Plumtree call at the house hoping to rent, having just returned from their honeymoon. Ollie persuades Stan to dress up as the butler and instructs him to tell them that the colonel isn't home. Stan however spots the policeman still on the prowl and lets the couple in. Things get tricky when they ask to see the master of the house, so Ollie disguises himself as the colonel. The ruse seems to be going well until the lady asks to see "Agnes" the maid. Stan is told by Ollie to put on the maid's uniform, and then has to explain that he's the only maid in the house at present, as all the others have left suffering from "housemaid's knees!" In fact, Stan plays such a convincing part that the lady persuades him to stay on and keep her company. Ollie and the Lord discuss rental terms while Stan changes back into the butler's clothes to play "Hives" the maid's supposed twin brother. The boys are about to leave the house, when the real colonel returns home having forgotten his bow and arrow. With their cover blown they hide in the trophy room, before making their exit dressed in a gnu skin. Closely followed by the police, the boys escape on a tandem, riding into a railway tunnel as a train enters at the other end. They emerge from the tunnel black and blue' and now riding unicycles.

After their first venture into feature films, the boys returned to what they did best, with this a re-working of their 1927 film DUCK SOUP. The film title ANOTHER FINE MESS was mistakenly taken from one of Ollie's catch phrases often mis-quoted, as Ollie never actually said it in any film. The correct terminology was in fact *'Well, here's another NICE mess you've gotten me into.'*

BE BIG

Directed by **James Parrott**, Produced by **Hal Roach**, Edited by **Richard Currier**, Filmed - Nov/Dec 1930, Released - Feb 7, 1931 by MGM, Running time - 3 reels.

With: **Isabelle Keith** (Mrs Hardy), **Anita Garvin** (Mrs Laurel), **Charlie Hall** (Bellboy), **Baldwin Cooke** (Pal from lodge, Cookie).

(Lola Marcel) 'Oh it can't be. What did he die of.' (Stan) 'I think he died of a Tuesday, or was it a Wednesday...' *(WAY OUT WEST)*

(Top) The classic soda fountain sketch from MEN O'WAR and below, the three wives from the regular and foreign releases of BLOTTO

Any Nuts?

(Top) Double the trouble in BRATS, and below Tiny Sandford points the way in PARDON US

What Was The Film When..?

Also appeared: Jack Hill, Ham Kinsey, Chet Brandenberg.

"Mr. Hardy is a man of great care, caution and discretion - Mr. Laurel is married too."

The Laurels and Hardys are about to leave for a weekend vacation to Atlantic City, when Ollie receives a phone call from a pal, telling him that the gang are holding a surprise stag party for him and Stan. Ollie informs him that he's not interested, until his friend tells him what is planned for the evening, reminding Ollie of the saying *'No man is bigger than the excuses he can make to his wife.'* He then rings off reminding Ollie to *'Be Big!'* With everybody ready to leave for the railway station, Ollie feigns illness, blaming it on the excitement of the forthcoming trip. He manages to persuade the wives to carry on with the vacation, promising that he and Stan will join them the next day. Ollie explains all to Stan, and they start to change into their lodge outfits. Their boots then become mixed up, with Ollie having great difficulty pulling Stan's much smaller pair on. He painfully realises his mistake, and tries in vain to remove them. Stan tries to help, succeeding only in dragging Ollie around the room, half wrecking the apartment in the process. Ollie gets a soaking when he falls into the bath, and as if that's not enough, the wives return home having missed the last train. The boys hide behind a wall bed, but are discovered by their angry partners, who fire shotguns at the pair, blowing them through the wall and into the street.

Sometimes a short would contain so much worthwhile material, that it would be extended into a three-reeler (their previous film ANOTHER FINE MESS being a prime example). Unfortunately BE BIG is not really improved by the addition of the third reel, and would have benefited from a shortening of the boot fitting/removing episode that dominates the film. It also contains a sketch taken from the silent film ANGORA LOVE (1929), where the boys try to hang their clothes on the same door hook.

CHICKENS COME HOME

Directed by **James Horne**, Produced by **Hal Roach**, Edited by **Richard Currier**, Filmed - Jan 1931, Released - Feb 21, 1931 by MGM, Running time - 3 reels.

Any Nuts?

With: **Mae Busch** (Blackmailer), **Thelma Todd** (Mrs Hardy), **Norma Drew** (Mrs Laurel), **James Finlayson** (Butler), **Patsy O'Byrne** ("Gossip"), **Frank Holliday** (Dinner guest), **Ham Kinsey, Baldwin Cooke, Dorothy Layton** (Office workers), **Charles French** (Judge), **Gertrude Pedlar** (Judge's wife).

Also appeared: Frank Rice, Gordon Douglas.

"Every man has a past - with some little 'indiscretion' he would like to bury - Mr. Laurel and Mr. Hardy have thirty or forty they would like to cremate."

Ollie is a successful fertiliser dealer who is running for mayor. He is reciting his acceptance speech to his general manager Stan, when an old flame (Mae Busch) enters the office and makes it quite clear she wants a share of his good fortune. Her blackmail demands are refused until she backs them up with a photograph of them together on the beach, taken when Ollie was "in his primrose days." When she threatens to tell all to the newspapers, Ollie agrees to meet her later that evening to discuss a settlement. Mrs Hardy then enters the office building, so Ollie's unwanted guest hides in the bathroom. Ollie is reminded by his wife of the dinner party they are holding that night, to be attended by some of the town's most influential people, which just happens to be taking place at the same time as Ollie's planned rendezvous. Later that evening, Stan is sent round to the blackmailer's apartment to stall her until Ollie can slip away from the party to make the pay-off. She is furious that Ollie has failed to show and despite Stan's attempts to keep her at bay by blocking up the front door, she escapes, intent on confronting Ollie at his home. Outside the apartment building, the blackmailer and Stan wrestle for the car keys but unfortunately for Stan, the town "gossip" sees them rolling about on the pavement and sets off for the Laurel household to tell his wife of the goings on. Stan and the blackmailer arrive at the dinner party as Ollie is entertaining the guests by singing at the piano. Ollie's old flame is introduced as Stan's wife, who then faints when Ollie threatens to shoot her. Mrs Hardy invites the "Laurels" to stay the night and goes off to prepare the guest room, giving the boys the opportunity to smuggle the unwanted intruder out of the house. When the real Mrs Laurel shows up armed with an axe and introduces herself to Mrs Hardy, the whole sham is blown and the boys are chased out of the house by Stan's axe-wielding wife.

(Title card) Give that baby a bath – then report to me to have your neck wrung (*SAILORS, BEWARE!*)

What Was The Film When..?

A virtual re-make of LOVE 'EM AND WEEP (1927) with Stan and Mae Busch playing their original roles. James Finlayson was demoted from his starring role in the silent film, to play the scheming butler. The film was released in Spanish as POLITQUERIAS, a six-reeler, with notable changes to the cast, including Linda Loredo as Mrs Hardy and Carmen Granada as Mrs Laurel.

THE STOLEN JOOLS

Directed by **William McGann**, Produced by **Pat Casey**, Filmed - Early 1931, Released - Apr 1931 by Paramount & National Screen Service, Running time - 2 reels.

With: **Eddie Kane** (Inspector Kane), **Wallace Beery** (Desk sergeant), **Buster Keaton** (Keystone Cop), **El Brendel** (Swedish waiter), **Gary Cooper** (Newspaper editor), **Maurice Chevalier** (Detective), **Joe E. Brown** (Man in false beard), **Gabby Hayes** (Projectionist).

Also appeared: The Our Gang Kids with Pete the pup, Polly Moran, Hedda Hopper, Edmund Lowe, Charlie Murray, George Sidney, Winnie Lightner, Fifi D'Orsay, Warner Baxter, Irene Dunne, Richard Dix, Eugene Pallette, Stu Erwin, Skeets Gallagher, Bebe Daniels, Ben Lyon, Jack Hill, Charles Rogers, Charles Butterworth (see also stars listed in storyline).

"T'was a balmy summer's evening - And all was quiet on the Western Coast - including Hollywood - Except at the SCREEN STARS ANNUAL BALL - Then came the dawn."

Norma Shearer has her jewels stolen while attending a celebrity party. The job of retrieving them is given to Inspector Kane, who arrives at the Shearer residence with his two best men, Stan and Ollie. The car pulls up outside and promptly falls to pieces. Ollie turns to Stan and says *'I told you not to make that last payment.'* Kane soon thinks he has the case wrapped when overhearing Joan Crawford admitting to the robbery to William Haines, but it turns out that all she has stolen is a little dog. After further investigations involving a lady (Dorothy

Any Nuts?

Lee) on a porch swing, Kane decides to go undercover in a diner, but is unable to get much sense out of his two suspects (Bert Wheeler and Robert Woolsey), who appear pre-occupied with slapping each other across the face. With the Inspector now in Sherlock Holmes guise, he targets Douglas Fairbanks Jnr. and Loretta Young, yet once again his search for the elusive jewels proves futile. Barbara Stanwyck reciting poetry, and Frank Fay don't escape Kane's attention, nor do Jack Oakie and Fay Wray, interrogated on a film set. Kane then thinks the mystery is solved when he catches Little Billy sneaking off to bury "The Stolen Jools" which turns out to be just a reel of film. Just then a small girl (Mitzi Green) calls Kane over and admits taking the jewels for safe keeping, after spotting Edward G. Robinson and George E. Stone hiding them in a drawer. With the mystery solved the girl ends the film with the moral of the story - *'Never spank a child on an empty stomach.'*

A promotional short intended to raise funds for research into tuberculosis and respiratory diseases. Every major studio loaned its stars (although the majority only appeared for a few seconds) with the costs of production met by Chesterfield Cigarettes and distributed free by Paramount. The opening credits boasted that more stars appeared than in any one film before. It was released in Britain a year later in 1932 under the title THE SLIPPERY PEARLS.

LAUGHING GRAVY

Directed by **James Horne**, Produced by **Hal Roach**, Edited by **Richard Currier**, Filmed - Feb 1931, Released - Apr 4, 1931 by MGM, Running time - 2 reels.

With: **Charlie Hall** (Landlord), **Charles Dorety** (Drunkard), **Harry Bernard** (Policeman).

Also appeared: Laughing Gravy the dog.

"Mr. Laurel and Mr. Hardy stuck together through thick and thin - one pocketbook between them, always empty."

(Ollie) 'We've got to raise a $100.' (Stan) '$100?' (Ollie) 'Yes.'
(Stan) 'We couldn't even raise a thousand.' *(ONE GOOD TURN)*

It's a cold winter's night and Stan is keeping everybody awake with an attack of the hiccoughs, including their dog Laughing Gravy, whom they are hiding in their rented room from their strict landlord. This causes the dog to start barking, which coupled with the bed collapsing, alerts the landlord, who discovers the dog and throws him outside into the snow. Ollie sneaks downstairs to retrieve their pet, but is locked out when the door blows shut behind him. Stan ties some bed sheets together and hauls the dog into the room. He tries to do the same for Ollie, only for the knot to slip and send Ollie falling into a freezing rain barrel. Stan goes downstairs to let Ollie back in to find him and his night-shirt frozen solid. When the bed collapses again, sending plaster crashing down onto the landlord in the room below, they hide Laughing Gravy up the chimney, where he clambers to the top and onto the snow covered roof. Stan follows and tries to pass him down to Ollie, who has eased himself out onto the window ledge. The window shuts, locking Ollie out, so Stan hauls him up onto the roof. With them now all stranded, they decide to climb back down the chimney. Stan and the dog make it safely down but Ollie slips and falls, bringing half of the stack down on top of him. Covered in soot, they decide to take a bath, just as the landlord walks in on them, and by chance gets the contents of the bath thrown all over him. He orders the boys to pack their bags, and they are about to vacate the premises, when a policeman arrives telling them that nobody is to leave, as the house is quarantined for two months due to an outbreak of smallpox. This proves too much for the landlord who makes a dramatic exit by shooting himself...twice!!

The idea for this film was taken from their earlier silent ANGORA LOVE. Due to a disagreement (?) with MGM, this was to be the last multi-lingual Laurel and Hardy picture, with future releases again reverting to be dubbed. LAUGHING GRAVY along with BE BIG plus additional material were all incorporated to produce a feature-length picture, with the French version entitled LES CAROTTIERS (Germaine de Neel as Mrs Hardy) running for six reels. The slightly longer Spanish version was called LOS CALAVERAS (Linda Loredo as Ollie's wife). An extant third reel was filmed but deleted in the English version.

OUR WIFE

Directed by **James Horne**, Produced by **Hal Roach**, Edited by **Richard Currier**, Filmed - Mar 1931, Released - May 16, 1931 by MGM, Running time - 2 reels.

Any Nuts?

With: **Jean "Babe" London** (Dulcy), **James Finlayson** (Dulcy's father), **Ben Turpin** (Justice of the Peace, William Gladding), **Blanche Payson** (Mrs Gladding), **Charley Rogers** (Butler).

> *"Mr. Hardy was making big preparations to get married -*
> *Mr. Laurel was taking a bath too."*

Ollie is about to marry his sweetheart Dulcy, but when her father sees Ollie's photograph, he forbids the marriage and locks his daughter in her bedroom. Dulcy rings Ollie telling him the bad news, who undeterred, plans a midnight elopement. On arriving at Dulcy's house, their plans are nearly scuppered when best man Stan rings the front door bell and informs the butler of the elopement. Dulcy's father rushes into her bedroom, where she is hiding behind the door. He is then locked in, while Dulcy sneaks downstairs to meet Ollie. Stan has hired the getaway car, but what should have been a limousine turns out to be a miniature Austin. After much huffing and puffing, Ollie and his equally large sweetheart eventually squeeze into the car, while Stan rides in the back with his head poking through the roof as they drive off. They wake the Justice of the Peace and ask him to perform the ceremony, with the cross-eyed official making a complete hash of it by marrying Ollie to Stan by mistake. He then asks permission to kiss the bride, and plants a smacker on Ollie!

Rotund actress "Babe" London had appeared with Stan in his solo career.

COME CLEAN

Directed by **James Horne**, Produced by **Hal Roach**, Edited by **Richard Currier**, Filmed - May 1931, Released - Sep 19, 1931 by MGM, Running time - 2 reels.

With: **Mae Busch** (Suicide case), **Gertrude Astor** (Mrs Hardy), **Linda Loredo** (Mrs Laurel), **Charlie Hall** (Ice cream parlour assistant), **Eddie Baker** (Detective), **Tiny Sandford** (Doorman), **Gordon Douglas** (Apartment desk clerk).

> *"Mr. Hardy holds that every husband should tell his wife the whole*
> *truth - Mr. Laurel is crazy too."*

What Was The Film When..?

All is bliss in the Hardy household, that is until the Laurels arrive at the door. While the wives make small talk, the boys head for the ice cream parlour to try and satisfy Stan's craving for chocolate ice cream. On the way back home they witness a lady jump into the river attempting to commit suicide, and between them they manage to drag her out. She is less than happy at being rescued and tells them that having saved her, they now have the responsibility of looking after her. All three arrive back at the Hardy apartment with Ollie pleading with the lady to leave them alone. She demands a pay-off so Ollie decides to "Come Clean" over the whole affair and tell the wives all. Unable to pluck up the courage, and against their better judgement, they hide her in the bedroom, as the wives become increasingly suspicious over their strange behaviour. Eventually Ollie pays her off with his wife's fur coat, but as the blackmailer is leaving the building, she is spotted by a detective and chased back up to the apartment, where she is locked in the bathroom with Stan. The detective breaks down the door to reveal Stan taking a bath fully clothed. The boys are asked who's accountable for bringing the lady into the apartment, with Ollie quick to pin all the blame on Stan. This however backfires as Stan is told he's to receive a $1,000 reward for her capture. When Stan tells Ollie of his intentions to spend all the reward money on chocolate ice cream, Ollie pulls out the plug and Stan disappears down the plug hole. Mrs Laurel enquires about her husbands whereabouts, with Ollie replying in his usual matter-of-fact manner 'he's gone to the beach!'

The opening scene was a re-working from the 1928 silent SHOULD MARRIED MEN GO HOME? Stan's wife in COME CLEAN was played by Linda Loredo, a frequent player in most of the Spanish versions of the Laurel and Hardy films.

ONE GOOD TURN

Directed by **James Horne**, Produced by **Hal Roach**, Edited by **Richard Currier**, Filmed - Jun 1931, Released - Oct 31, 1931 by MGM, Running time - 2 reels.

With: **Mary Carr** (Old lady), **James Finlayson**, **Lyle Tayo**, **Dorothy Granger**, **Snub Pollard**, **Gordon Douglas** (Amateur players), **Billy Gilbert** (Drunkard).

Any Nuts?

Also appeared: Dick Gilbert, George Miller, Baldwin Cooke, Ham Kinsey, Retta Palmer, Charley Young, William Gillespie.

"Seeing America! Mr. Laurel and Mr. Hardy have cast off all financial worries - Total assests - One Ford, Model 1911 - One tent, Model 1861 - One Union suit, two shirts and three socks."

The boys are victims of the depression, travelling the countryside in their battered old car. When Stan burns down their tent and ruins the supper, they are forced to beg for food. They knock at the door of an old lady, telling her that they haven't eaten for three whole days - yesterday, today and tomorrow! She takes pity on them and agrees to make them a meal, while the boys chop her some wood. While tucking into their meal, the boys overhear some amateur dramatics taking place in the next room. The old lady is playing the part of a harassed home owner unable to pay the ruthless rent collector (James Finlayson) $100, as her money has been stolen. Stan and Ollie think the situation is for real and head off to town to sell their only worthwhile possession - their car - to the highest bidder. Ollie has soon gathered a large crowd and a drunk bids the $100 required. He takes the money out of his wallet but puts the wallet into Stan's pocket by mistake. Ollie is just about to close the bidding, when a partially deaf bystander asks Stan the time. Stan shouts out *'one twenty-five,'* and believing this to be an improved bid, Ollie sells the car to Stan, whose newly acquired wallet becomes the centre of attention. When Stan can't explain where the wallet is from, Ollie accuses him of stealing it from the old lady. Despite his innocent pleas, Ollie manhandles Stan into the car, which duly collapses in a heap. Stan is dragged back to the old lady's house where Ollie tells her he has nabbed the robber. Somewhat bemused by this, she explains that they had only been rehearsing for the community play. Ollie sheepishly apologises to his buddy, but Stan will have none of it, and sets about him before chasing him into the wood house.

First appearance of Billy Gilbert (born William Gilbert Baron, Louisville, 1894), who was signed up by Hal Roach on Stan's recommendation. He went on to enjoy a distinguished career playing alongside such established artists as The Three Stooges, Wheeler and Woolsey, The Marx Brothers, W. C. Fields, Charlie Chaplin, Buster Keaton and Charley Chase. He would appear in ten Laurel and Hardy films, with his most prominent role being Professor Theodore von

What Was The Film When..?

Schwarzenhoffen in the Oscar-winning THE MUSIC BOX. Stan's final moments of madness in ONE GOOD TURN, where for once Ollie is the bullied party, were specifically written for Stan's young daughter Lois. She had developed quite an aversion for her "Uncle Babe" (Ollie) whenever he visited the Laurel household, believing all the bullying endured by her father at the hands of Ollie while filming to be for real.

BEAU HUNKS

Directed by **James Horne**, Produced by **Hal Roach**, Edited by **Richard Currier**, Filmed - Sep 1931, Released - Dec 12, 1931 by MGM, Running time - 4 reels.

With: **Charles Middleton** (Commandant), **James Horne** (Abdul Kasim K'Horne), **Tiny Sandford** (Legionnaire officer), **Charlie Hall** (New recruit No.13), **Leo Willis** (New recruit), **Harry Schultz** (Captain Schultz), **Broderick O'Farrell** (Commander at Fort Arid), **Jean Harlow** (As Jeanie Weenie in photograph only).

Also appeared: Gordon Douglas, Sam Lufkin, Marvin Hatley, Jack Hill, Bob Kortman, Baldwin Cooke, Dick Gilbert, Oscar Morgan, Ham Kinsey.

"Love comes: Mr. Hardy is at last conscious of the grand passion - Mr. Laurel isn't even conscious of the Grand Canyon."

Ollie is hopelessly in love with his sweetheart Jeanie Weenie, a lady who has travelled the world and loved by everyone. He informs Stan that he's soon to be married, but his dreams are shattered when he receives a letter from her telling him the romance is all over as she loves another. Realising what a big sucker he's been, Ollie decides the only way to forget the tragic love affair is to join the Foreign Legion and take Stan along too! On arriving at the barracks they notice other heartbroken legionnaires grieving over Jeanie's photograph as well. The boys march into the commandant's office telling him of their wish to leave, but he will have none of it and to make matters worse, there on his office wall is a photo of Jeanie. Along with the other recruits they are sent out on a tortuous eight hour training march. When they return Stan is so tired he tells Ollie that he's feels just like Jeanie Weenie - as though he's travelled all over the world! They are settling down to some much needed rest,

(Stan) 'What's the matter?' (Ollie) 'I don't know.' (Stan) 'I know.' (Ollie) 'What?'
(Stan)'Your in love.' (Ollie) 'In what?' (Stan) 'In love, l-u-g-h love.' *(SWISS MISS)*

Any Nuts?

when they are ordered to assemble as the commandant has been informed of an attack by the Riffs on Fort Arid, another Legion post. Next day and still on the march, a sand storm blows up and the boys become separated from the main party. At Fort Arid they have all but given up hope after suffering a twenty day siege, yet things seem to look up when they think the relief party has arrived. They open the gates expecting to welcome their liberators, but find just Stan and Ollie instead. The boys are put to work patrolling the walls just as the Riffs storm the fort. Somehow Stan and Ollie manage to turn the inevitable defeat into victory by sprinkling tacks all over the fort floor, rendering the bare-footed enemy helpless. The relief party turn up as the boys arrest the Riff leader, Abdul Kasim K'Horne, who when searched, is found to possess a photo of Jeanie as well.

Director James Horne (born San Francisco, 1881) also appeared in front of the camera, playing "Chief of the Riff-Raff" Abdul (Abul?) Kasim K'Horne, carrying off the role with great aplomb. Charles Middleton made the first of his four appearances with the boys, before going on to greater things playing Ming the Merciless in the Flash Gordon series. BEAU HUNKS fell into the category between short and feature length film and was Stan and Ollie's only four reel picture (excluding foreign releases and the US version of A CHUMP AT OXFORD) and was released in Britain under the slightly different title BEAU CHUMPS. Several parts in the picture were lifted from previous films, including Ollie massaging Stan's foot believing it to be his own aching limb, originally done in the 1929 silent ANGORA LOVE and the hat routine performed in the commandant's office, was also a re-working of the gag from BACON GRABBERS.

ON THE LOOSE

Directed by **Hal Roach**, Produced by **Hal Roach**, Edited by **Richard Currier**, Filmed - Sep 1931, Released - Dec 26, 1931 by MGM, Running time - 2 reels.

With: **Thelma Todd** (Fed up girlfriend), **ZaSu Pitts** (Her roommate), **Claud Allister** (English gentleman), **John Loder** (Gentleman's pal), **Billy Gilbert** (Pierre at the boutique), **Charlie Hall** (Shooting gallery attendant), **Otto Fries** (Bully at funfair).

What Was The Film When..?

Also appeared: Gordon Douglas, Jack Hill, Buddy MacDonald.

Two girlfriends return home exhausted after a day out at Coney Island, vowing never to return, as it's the only place their boyfriends ever seem to take them. Next day whilst strolling down the street, they are splashed with mud as a car speeds past. The driver, an English gentleman, apologises and takes the girls to a boutique to buy them new outfits. All dressed up with nowhere to go, the girls are invited to accompany the gentleman and friend to an exciting and original day out at the weekend. They gladly accept, but come Saturday, their enthusiasm is dampened somewhat when they arrive at their destination - Coney Island! After several rides on the roller coaster and target practice at the shooting gallery, the next stop is the fun house, where the foursome clash with a bully and his girl. Battered and bruised, the girls arrive home and are licking their wounds when Stan and Ollie call at the apartment, enquiring if they would fancy a day out....to Coney Island!! This is the final straw, and the boys are sent running for cover as the girls chase them out of the apartment hurling Coney Island souvenirs at them.

Cameo appearance time for the boys in this Thelma Todd/ZaSu Pitts short, written, directed and produced by Hal Roach himself.

HELPMATES

Directed by **James Parrott**, Produced by **Hal Roach**, Edited by **Richard Currier**, Filmed - Oct 1931, Released - Jan 23, 1932 by MGM, Running time - 2 reels.

With: **Blanche Payson** (Mrs Hardy), **Robert Callahan** (Telegram boy), **Bobby Burns** (Gardener).

"When the cat's away - the mice start looking up telephone numbers."

With his wife away in Chicago visiting her mother, Ollie throws a wild party, where he loses all his money in a poker game. Next day, and with the house turned upside down, he receives a telegram informing him that his wife will be home by noon that day. In a panic he telephones Stan, who had missed the party because of a dog bite, and asks him to call round to help with the tidying up. Stan

Any Nuts?

arrives and begins by washing the dishes, as Ollie changes into his suit to meet his wife at the railway station. A series of mishap's result in Ollie covered in soot and flour, but his next change of clothes fares no better, when Stan, trying to get rid of the washing-up water from the blocked sink, soaks him through. The wet clothes are put in front of the gas stove to dry, but the kitchen blows up after Ollie tries to light it. He then has to put on the only set of clothes he has left, a navy uniform, with plumed hat, sword and all, surprising Stan so much by his appearance, that he salutes him when he walks into the room. Ollie leaves for the railway station, while Stan finishes the tidying up. One hour later Ollie returns alone and sporting a black eye, to find the house a burned out shell. Stan tearfully explains about the welcome home fire he was preparing, which had got out of hand after pouring paraffin on it. As Stan leaves, Ollie asks him to shut the door behind him, virtually the only part of the house left standing, before sitting in an armchair. The final slap in the face comes for Ollie when the heavens open, soaking him through.

ANY OLD PORT

Directed by James Horne, **Produced by** Hal Roach, **Edited by** Richard Currier, **Filmed** - Nov 1931, **Released** - Mar 5, 1932 by MGM, **Running Time** - 2 reels.

With: **Walter Long** (Mugsie Long), **Jacqueline Wells** (Cleaning girl), **Harry Bernard** (Fight promoter), **Bobby Burns** (Justice of the Peace), **Charlie Hall** (Stan's second), **Sam Lufkin** (Referee), **Dick Gilbert** (Long's second), **Will Stanton** (Ringside drunk).

Also appeared: Eddie Baker, Jack Hill, Baldwin Cooke, Ed Brandenberg.

"In port - Mr. Laurel and Mr. Hardy were just home from a whaling voyage - Mr. Hardy shipped as head harpooner - Mr. Laurel went along as bait."

The boys are sailors on shore leave, and book into Ye Mariner's Rest, a rough and ready hotel, where Stan asks for a room with a Southern explosion! They learn that the proprietor, Mugsie Long, is forcing his cleaning girl to marry him. The girl pleads with the boys for help, before being locked in the store room. Stan and Ollie decide to sort Mugsie out, only to realise that they

---

(Stan) 'I've waited on ya with your hands and feet...' (*THE FLYING DEUCES*)

have bitten off more than they can chew when the pool balls they throw bounce off his head without any effect. The Justice of the Peace arrives to perform the marriage ceremony, but Stan and Ollie refuse point blank to act as witnesses, and steal the store room key. A mad scramble for the key follows as they are chased around the hotel. Stan manages to unlock the door and let the girl go free, as the chase continues outside, where Mugsie falls off the quayside and into the dock, swearing revenge if he ever meets up with the boys again. With their money still in the hotel, the boys contemplate their bleak prospects, until Ollie bumps into an old pal who runs a boxing stadium down the road. He promises them $50 for a four round preliminary fight later that evening, which Ollie readily agrees to as he won't be the one fighting. Come fight time, Stan climbs into the ring to face of all people Mugsie Long, who sends his second to load one of his gloves with nuts and bolts. The fight begins and when the pair become entangled, Stan finds himself in possession of the loaded glove. He chases Mugsie around the ring, much to the disbelief of Ollie who has bet all of the purse money with a drunken spectator on Stan losing. Mugsie tries to snatch back the glove and duly knock himself out. Stan is declared the winner, as Mugsie's second informs a policeman of the loaded glove. Stan learns about the purse money and draws back his glove to sock Ollie, only to knock out the advancing policeman instead.

THE MUSIC BOX

Directed by **James Parrott**, Produced by **Hal Roach**, Edited by **Richard Currier**, Filmed - Dec 1931, Released - Apr 16, 1932 by MGM, Running time - 3 reels.

With: **Billy Gilbert** (Professor Theodore von Schwarzenhoffen M.D., A.D., D.D.S., F.L.D., F.F.F., und F.), **Gladys Gale** (Professor's wife), **Sam Lufkin** (Policeman), **Charlie Hall** (Postman), **Lilyan Irene** (Children's nanny), **William Gillespie** (Piano salesman).

Also appeared: Susie the horse.

> *"Mr. Laurel and Mr. Hardy decided to re-organize and re-supervise their entire financial structure - So they took the $3.80 and went into business."*

Any Nuts?

'*Tall Oaks From Little Acorns Grow.*' That's the motto of the Laurel and Hardy Transfer Company, who are dispatched to 1127, Walnut Avenue to deliver a piano. The house is situated at the top of a large flight of steps, so with great difficulty they start to haul the piano to the top. After a set-to with a children's nanny and a policeman and with the piano back at the bottom of the steps, they start all over again to lug the piano back upwards. Half way to achieving the task, Professor Theodore von Schwarzenhoffen, a high and mighty fellow, asks the boys to move it out of the way as he refuses to walk round. Stan further enrages the professor when he knocks his top hat off, sending it flying down the steps, where it is flattened by a truck. Finally after a great deal of effort, the summit is reached, only for a postman to tell them that all their efforts could have been spared as there is a road leading directly to the house. Without another thought, the boys drag the piano back down the steps, so they can bring it back up again by road! With nobody at home, they use a block and tackle to pull the piano through an upstairs window. The house is soon turned into a shambles as they try and set it up in the front room. They are in the middle of cleaning up the mess, when the owner of the house, the professor himself, arrives home. He insists that the piano cannot be his as he detests them, and to prove his point, he smashes it to pieces with an axe. Just then his wife returns home and tells him that the piano was bought as a surprise birthday present for him. He immediately apologises to the boys for the unfortunate misunderstanding, as Stan hands him a fountain pen to sign for the delivery. The rapport however is soon over, as the pen spurts ink into the professor's face.

One of Laurel and Hardy's most loved and recollected pictures. Stan and Ollie were rewarded for all their puffing and panting, when THE MUSIC BOX, based on the storyline from HATS OFF (1927), was awarded an Oscar for the newly created category of Best Live Action Short Comedy Subject of 1931-32. For the record, the steps used in both films numbered 131, and can still be found today on Vendome Street in the Silver Lake district of Los Angeles. The steps would feature in other films, including AN ACHE IN EVERY STAKE starring The Three Stooges, who are given the job of delivering blocks of ice up the famous steps.

(Stan) 'Is that you Fanny?' (Fanny) 'Yes.' (Stan) 'Say listen, Ollie wants to take us out tonight to celebrate our university.' *(TWICE TWO)*

What Was The Film When..?

THE CHIMP

Directed by **James Parrott**, Produced by **Hal Roach**, Edited by **Richard Currier**, Filmed - Jan/Feb 1932, Released - May 21, 1932 by MGM, Running time - 3 reels.

With: **Charles Gemora** (The Chimp), **Billy Gilbert** (Joe the landlord), **James Finlayson** (Circus ringmaster), **Martha Sleeper** (Landlord's wife, Ethel), **Bobby Burns** (Hotel guest), **Tiny Sandford** ("Destructo the Cannonball King"), **George Miller** (Circus owner), **Dorothy Granger** (As Ethel, the landlord's wife in photograph only).

Also appeared: Jack Hill, Baldwin Cooke, Belle Hare, Dorothy Layton.

"Mr. Hardy's aesthetic nature thrilled at the beauties of circus life - Mr. Laurel never got any further than the monkey cage."

Stan and Ollie are stage hands in a circus that goes bust, so the owner decides to give each of his employees a part of the show. Stan draws the flea circus, while Ollie gets the star attraction of the show, Ethel "The Human Chimpanzee." They are chased from the circus grounds by an escaped lion and take refuge in a small hotel, whose owner is angry with his wife, also called Ethel, for failing to return home that night, leading him to suspect that she is playing around. The boys are given a room for the night while the chimp, locked outside, climbs the drainpipe and enters their room, stealing the bedclothes from Ollie's bed. Ollie gets in with Stan, but sleep is out of the question as the fleas have escaped and are inhabiting the bed. When the chimp hears music being played by another guest (Bobby Burns), she starts to dance around the room. The landlord hears the boys ordering Ethel back to bed, and thinking they are talking to his wife, is filled with jealousy and bursts into the room brandishing a pistol. He pours his heart out to the chimp hiding under the bedclothes, believing it to be his wife, only realising the error when his wife walks in on them. The ape is ordered out of the hotel, so she grabs the pistol, sending everyone running for cover.

Any Nuts ?

Billy Gilbert
1894 - 1971

What Was The Film When..?

COUNTY HOSPITAL

Directed by **James Parrott**, Produced by **Hal Roach**, Edited by **Bert Jordan & Richard Currier**, Filmed - Feb 1932, Released - Jun 25, 1932 by MGM, Running time - 2 reels.

With: **Billy Gilbert** (Doctor), **May Wallace, Dorothy Layton, Lilyan Irene, Belle Hare** (Nurses), **William Austin** (Ollie's roommate), **Sam Lufkin** (Policeman).

Also appeared: Baldwin Cooke, Ham Kinsey, Frank Holliday.

"Mr. Hardy fell on his leg and was laid up for two months. Mr. Laurel fell on his head - and hadn't felt better in years."

With nothing else to do, Stan decides to visit Ollie recuperating in hospital after injuring his leg. Ollie meanwhile, is enjoying the peace of hospital life, so Stan's visit and his present of hard boiled eggs and nuts are not entirely appreciated. Ollie's hopes of a box of candy are dashed when Stan tells him that they are too expensive and that he didn't pay him for the last box! Stan tucks into the eggs himself, but has little success in cracking the nuts. Ollie is cheered considerably when the doctor calls on his rounds and tells him he'll be hospitalised for at least another two months. Stan then spots a weight on the floor, and picks it up to crack open the nuts, unaware that it's attached to a cord suspending Ollie's injured leg. The doctor makes a grab for the weight only to fall through the top floor window, clinging to the weight for dear life while Ollie is suspended in mid-air. The doctor scrambles to safety just as the cord snaps, sending Ollie crashing down onto the bed. After he is ordered to leave, Ollie has difficulty in pulling on his trousers over the heavily bandaged leg, so Stan cuts off the trouser leg only to snip off the wrong one. Just then Ollie's roommate enters in a jovial mood having been told he can go home. He too starts to dress before realising he is wearing Ollie's trousers, with his own now resembling a pair of shorts. Stan then sits down on a syringe containing enough sedative to make him sleep for a month. The boys leave hospital and climb aboard the car with Stan at the wheel as the sedative starts to take effect. Ollie is increasingly concerned by Stan's erratic driving as he becomes drowsy at the wheel. After several close

(Ollie) 'Bring us two tankards of your rarest vintage.' (Waiter) 'Yes sir.'
(Stan) 'Yeh and put a wallop in it it.' *(THE BOHEMIAN GIRL)*

Any Nuts?

calls, the inevitable accident happens and they are hit by a tram, bending the car at right angles. A policeman spots the incident and orders Stan to pull over, but despite his best efforts, he is unable to obey the cop's request as the car drives round in circles.

PACK UP YOUR TROUBLES

Directed by **George Marshall** & **Raymond McCarey***, Produced by **Hal Roach**, Edited by **Richard Currier**, Filmed - May 1932, Released - Sep 17, 1932 by MGM, Running time - 68 minutes. *credited only

With: **Donald Dillaway** (Eddie Smith), **Jacquie Lyn** (Eddie's daughter), **James Finlayson** (The general), **Richard Tucker** (Bank president/Eddie's father), **Charles Middleton** (Welfare officer), **Rychard Cramer** (Evil foster parent, Uncle Jack), **Adele Watson** (Foster parent, Annie), **Frank Brownlee** (Drill sergeant), **George Marshall** (Army cook/Pierre the chef), **Muriel Evans** (The bride), **Billy Gilbert** (Bride's father, Mr. Hathaway), **Grady Sutton** (Eddie the groom), **C. Montague Shaw** (Groom's father), **Charley Rogers** (Colonel's valet Rogers who has a cold), **James Morton** (Policeman), **Mary Carr** (Lady who delivers letter to Eddie), **Tom Kennedy** (Recruiting officer), **Mary Gordon** (Mrs MacTavish), **Ellinor Vanderveer** (Wedding guest), **Frank Rice** (Parkins the butler), **Nora Cecil** (Welfare assistant), **Charlie Hall** (Worker by dumb waiter).

Also appeared: Al Hallet, Bill O'Brien, Lew Kelly, Bud Fine, Jack Hill, Dorothy Layton, Marvin Hatley, Baldwin Cooke, Robert Emmett Homans, Bob O'Conor, George Miller, Chet Brandenberg, Ham Kinsey.

*"April 1917 - When the scratch of a pen
on Capitol Hill caused crowns to rattle."*

Browbeaten into the army during America's entry into World War One, the boys' arrival at training camp soon upsets the drill sergeant, who puts them to work emptying garbage cans as punishment. When the cook sarcastically tells them to take the garbage to the general, they do just that, and all the rubbish ends up on his floor. They are sent to "the slammer" along with the cook who promises to get even with them for snitching on him. Stan and Ollie

(Stan) 'Your right, self reservation is the last law of average.' (*SAPS AT SEA*)

are posted to the front with their good buddy Eddie Smith, who is killed one night during an enemy raid. The boys are sent out to capture a prisoner in return, having been volunteered for the job by the sergeant in the trenches. They take shelter from the exploding shells in a tank and by a sheer fluke, capture the whole of the enemy unit. Armistice arrives and the boys set out to find Eddie's baby girl. They snatch her from ruthless foster parents and try to find her grandparents. This proves to be a difficult task, due to the vast number of "Smiths" in New York. Armed with a city directory, they arrive at 311, Chester Drive where a wedding is about to take place. When the bride's father hears that they have Eddie's baby in tow (the groom is also called Eddie), he thinks a major scandal is about to break and the wedding is called off. Only when the misunderstanding is resolved do the boys get their comeuppance, and are chased from the premises by the bride's father armed with his Winchester. Deciding to continue the search by telephone from the safety of their rented room, the boys still draw a blank in their quest to locate the little girl's elusive grandparents. One day while working on their lunch wagon, they are paid a visit by a welfare officer who promises to have the girl put in an orphanage. The boys decide to move to another state and go to the bank to re-finance their lunch business. The bank president though refuses their application, stating that he would have to be knocked cold before lending that amount of money. He then leans back in his chair and dislodges a statuette behind him thus rendering him unconscious. The boys take him for his word and reluctantly take the money, but are soon captured and taken to the bank president's home for identification. As the boys empty their pockets, the president notices a photograph of them together with Eddie, who turns out to be his son. With the long search over, and the little girl in her new home, all seemingly ends happily as the boys are released without charge. They are invited to stay for dinner, but when Pierre the chef - alias their old army cook - spots them, the dinner date is broken, as he runs them out the house.

Stan and Ollie's second venture into feature films, with director George Marshall making a rare appearance in front of the camera as the army cook, and later in the film as Pierre the chef. The film contains the hilarious scene where Jacquie Lyn sends Stan to sleep reading *him* Goldilocks and the Three Bears!

Any Nuts ?

SCRAM!

Directed by **Raymond McCarey**, Produced by **Hal Roach**, Edited by **Richard Currier**, Filmed - Jun 1932, Released - Sep 10, 1932 by MGM, Running time - 2 reels.

With: **Rychard Cramer** (Judge Beaumont), **Arthur Housman** (Drunkard), **Vivien Oakland** (Mrs Beaumont), **Charles McMurphy** (Policeman on beat), **Sam Lufkin** (Policeman in court), **Baldwin Cooke** (Court reporter), **Charles Dorety** (Man awaiting trial).

Stan and Ollie are up in front of the judge on a vagrancy charge and only escape a hundred and eighty day jail sentence because all the jails are full. The judge, who has a particular dislike for tramps and drunks, gives them just one hour to get out of town. Walking out into the pouring rain they notice an inebriated gent looking for his car key which has fallen down a pavement grating. After helping him recover it, they are rewarded with the promise of a bed for the night. At the house the boys are invited to go upstairs and make themselves comfortable, while their drunken friend puts his car away. He returns and prepares himself a night-cap by filling a water jug with gin and is half way up the stairs when he is challenged by the butler. Realising he is at the wrong address he leaves. Meanwhile the boys have made themselves at home but become concerned when their friend fails to return. They are about to look for him when they bump into the lady of the house. Confronted by two complete strangers she faints, so the boys try to revive her with a drink of what they think is water from the jug. The lady is soon quite tipsy and starts dancing and wrestling with the boys who are reluctant to take part in her games. When she develops the hiccoughs, Stan fetches her another glass of "water" and is seen pouring the drink by the real owner of the house, Judge Beaumont, the very fellow who ordered them out of town. He realises what's in the jug and walks into the bedroom to see Stan apparently plying his wife with booze. Stan, Ollie and Mrs Beaumont are sitting on the bed in fits of laughter, which subsides when they spot the judge with murder in his eyes. Suddenly the lights go out and all hell breaks loose.

Arthur Housman (born New York, October 10, 1890) made the first of his five appearances with the boys, playing what would become his customary and extremely convincing role as a drunk. After the film

(Note on door from Stan) Sorry you're out. If I don't come back I won't be here – Stan.
(COME CLEAN)

What Was The Film When..?

Tired recruits in PACK UP YOUR TROUBLES

Jacquie Lyn is the centre of attention in PACK UP YOUR TROUBLES

What Was The Film When..?

(Top) Mae Busch as the blackmailer in CHICKENS COME HOME and below the boys tangle with Walter Long in ANY OLD PORT

Any Nuts?

(Top) Charlie Hall in typical mood in LAUGHING GRAVY and below
(from left to right) Ben Turpin, Fay Holderness, and Jean "Babe" London in OUR WIFE

What Was The Film When..?

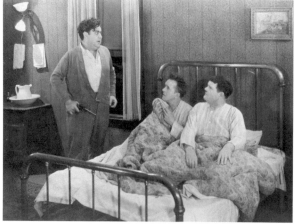

(Top) Landlord Billy Gilbert in THE CHIMP
and below Mae Busch, Gertrude Astor and Linda Loredo in COME CLEAN

Any Nuts?

was in the can, the boys decided to holiday together. Ollie joined Stan in England visiting his father and stepmother. It was only Stan's second visit back home since he had left with the Karno troupe in 1912 (he had returned briefly in 1927). Ollie was hoping to play a few rounds on the golf courses of England and Scotland but the holiday was turned into a massive publicity stunt organised by MGM. The boys were dumbstruck with the reception they received on arrival and the mass hysteria encountered wherever they visited, as Laurel and Hardy mania gripped Britain. Ollie managed only a few games of golf and the welcoming crowds in Glasgow were so large, that several people were hurt upon their arrival, with Stan and Ollie themselves nearly crushed to death. The vacation and much needed rest they sought were out of the question. Maybe an ocean voyage or a trip into the mountains would have been a better alternative! (see SONS OF THE DESERT and THEM THAR HILLS.)

THEIR FIRST MISTAKE

Directed by **George Marshall**, Produced by **Hal Roach**, Edited by **Richard Currier**, Filmed - Sep 1932, Released - Nov 5, 1932 by MGM, Running time - 2 reels.

With: **Mae Busch** (Mrs Arabella Hardy), **Billy Gilbert** (Server of writ), **George Marshall** (Neighbour).

"Mr. Hardy was married - Mr. Laurel was also unhappy."

Mrs Hardy is less than pleased with her husband for spending so much of his time with Mr. Laurel. When Stan phones Ollie about a night out at the Cement Worker's Bazaar, Ollie pretends that it's his boss, Mr. Jones, inviting him out to a business meeting. For once Ollie is in his wife's good books, that is until Stan calls round to tell them it was him on the telephone. Ollie is carpet beaten out of the apartment and runs across the hall to Stan's room. Stan suggests that a baby in the house would be a good idea to keep his wife occupied, leaving them to go out whenever they choose. Ollie agrees and goes out to adopt, returning home with a beautiful bouncing baby, only to find that his wife has left home, suing him for divorce and Stan for alienation of her husband's affections. The boys spend a sleepless night trying to get the baby to stop crying. This proves difficult as the neighbours keep telephoning,

(Ollie) 'Call me a cab.' (Stan) 'You're a cab.' *(ANOTHER FINE MESS)*

complaining about the noise. Stan feeds the baby a bottle of milk, and this seems to do the trick, until Ollie trips over the lamp stand flex and crashes into the kitchen. They all retire to bed with Ollie doing his best to stop the crying, by singing and feeding the baby whilst trying to sleep himself. This has little effect, and when Ollie wakes he realises why, as he has been feeding the milk to Stan instead.

TOWED IN A HOLE

Directed by **George Marshall**, Produced by **Hal Roach**, Edited by **Richard Currier**, Filmed - Nov 1932, Released - Dec 31, 1932 by MGM, Running time - 2 reels.

With: **Billy Gilbert** (Junk yard owner).

For a change the boys are doing well for themselves with their own small business selling fresh fish. While out on their rounds, Stan comes up with an idea to make even more money by catching their own, so that everything sold would be clear profit. With a million dollar idea like that, Ollie decides to buy a boat. At Joe's Junk Yard, the boys make their new investment shipshape. Stan fills the boat with water to find the leaks while Ollie gives it a new coat of paint. Due to Stan's antics, Ollie is soon wearing more of the paint than the boat. They take it in turns soaking each other, until they realise their childish squabble is getting them nowhere. They shake hands and make up, but the truce is soon broken when Ollie slips on a cake of soap left on deck and dives headfirst into a pool of paint. While Ollie continues to mend the leaks, Stan and the anchor he is scrubbing, crash through the bottom of the boat. Stan is banished below deck, but even then Ollie isn't safe. Trying to amuse himself, Stan gets his head stuck between the base of the mast and the cabin wall. He tries to free himself by sawing the mast in half, unaware that Ollie is up a ladder painting the top half of it. The mast breaks, with Ollie splashing down into a pool of water. Eventually the work is completed, due mainly to Stan being banned from helping. When they try to tow the boat away it proves too heavy, so Stan suggests they put up the sail. The sail fills with wind and pushes the boat and the car down a slope where both are smashed to pieces at the bottom.

Any Nuts ?

TWICE TWO

Directed by **James Parrott**, Produced by **Hal Roach**, Edited by **Bert Jordan**, Filmed - Nov 1932, Released - Feb 25, 1933 by MGM, Running time - 2 reels.

With: **Stan Laurel** (Mrs Hardy), **Oliver Hardy** (Mrs Fanny Laurel), **Charlie Hall** (Delivery man), **Baldwin Cooke** (Shop assistant), **Carol Tevis** (Voice-over for Mrs Hardy), **May Wallace** (Voice-over for Mrs Laurel).

Believe it or not, Ollie is a brain specialist and Stan his associate advisor working on the switchboard. Each has married the other's sister, and on this particular day are celebrating their first wedding anniversaries. The girls have planned a dinner party at the Laurels but Stan's sister, as accident prone as her brother, ruins Ollie's surprise cake. The boys arrive home from the office and Stan is sent out with fifteen cents to buy some strawberry ice cream. The shop is out of that particular flavour so Stan rings home to ask which other to buy. The shop is also out of tutti frutti and chocolate before Stan realises that he's in the wrong shop, by which time he has to return home having spent all his money on phone calls! An argument breaks out over dinner regarding table manners, and when they start insulting each other's families, Ollie and wife decide to eat elsewhere. They are just about to leave when a delivery man calls with another cake. He asks Mrs Hardy to make sure that Mrs Laurel gets it, and only too happy to oblige, she splats it straight into her face.

Stan and Ollie again played dual roles as they had done previously in BRATS. This was to be James Parrott's 22nd and last time in the director's chair for a Laurel and Hardy film.

FRA DIAVOLO (THE DEVIL'S BROTHER)

Directed by **Hal Roach** & **Charles Rogers**, Produced by **Hal Roach**, Edited by **Bert Jordan** & **William Terhune**, Filmed - Feb/Mar 1933, Released - May 5, 1933 by MGM, Running time - 90 minutes.

With: **Dennis King** (Fra Diavolo/Marquis de San Marco), **Thelma Todd** (Lady Pamela Rocburg), **James Finlayson** (Lord Rocburg), **Lucille Browne** (Zerlina), **Arthur Pierson** (Captain Lorenzo),

(Stan) 'Can you beat that?' (Ollie) 'What?' (Stan) 'What a terrible catsafterme.' *(ANY OLD PORT)*

What Was The Film When..?

Henry Armetta (The innkeeper, Matteo), **Matt McHugh** (Francesco), **Lane Chandler** (Lieutenant), **Nina Quartaro** (Rita), **James Morton** ("Deaf" woodcutter).

Also appeared: George Miller, Tiny Sandford, Jack Hill, Dick Gilbert, Rolfe Sedan, Kay Deslys, Leo Willis, Lillian Moore, Walter Shumway, Louise Carver, Harry Bernard.

> *"In the early 18th century, Northern Italy was terrorized by bandits. Boldest among the robber chieftains was Fra Diavolo (The "Devil's Brother") who masqueraded as the elegant Marquis de San Marco in order to mingle with the rich nobility and locate their wealth. Great Lords lost their gold to him. Great Ladies their hearts."*

Stanlio and Ollio are wandering the mountain trails when they are held up by masked bandits and robbed of their life savings. Stan comes up with the idea of becoming bandits themselves to recoup their losses. Their first intended victim, a partially deaf woodcutter, spins them such a sad tale, they end up handing him some money instead! Their next target turns out to be none other than the notorious bandit Fra Diavolo, with Ollie proudly boasting that he himself is the bandit king. Surrounded by Diavolo's band of cut throats, the boys are sentenced to be hanged, until Stan's tearful plea lands him the job as Ollie's executioner! Diavolo inspects the haul of booty stolen by his gang from Lord and Lady Rocburg, a couple he had travelled with while posing as the Marquis de San Marco. He is less than happy to find that the 500,000 francs the Rocburg's had in their possession are not among the haul, so decides to finish the job himself. He reprieves Ollie and hires the boys as his personal servants while again posing as the Marquis. They arrive at La Taverna del CuCu, where the rich couple are staying, with Diavolo hoping to woo Lady Pamela and find the whereabouts of her husband's fortune, and it isn't long before his charming manner has her under his spell. Stan and Ollie are sent to Lord Rocburg's room with a glass of wine spiked with strong sleeping powders. The gesture however is flatly refused so Stan, fearful of spilling the good vintage, gulps it down instead. Diavolo gives the boys their orders for the night as Stan starts to feel the effects of the wine. Diavolo enters the Rocburg's room, but the

Any Nuts?

robbery is interrupted by the return of the guard, who have discovered the bandit hideout and killed twenty of his men. Next day at the tavern, Zerlina, the innkeeper's daughter is due to marry Francesco, a rich nobleman, with the marriage only taking place to please Zerlina's father who wants her to marry into money. Her real love is Captain Lorenzo who has been trying in vain to capture Diavolo so he can claim not only the reward but Zerlina's hand as well. The boys are sent down to the cellar to fetch wine, with Stan consuming more than his fair share. Meanwhile Diavolo tricks Lady Pamela into revealing the hidden cash that is sewn into the layers of her silk petticoat. Diavolo swears his undying love and persuades her to slip into something more comfortable, giving him the chance to steal the petticoat. Stan's drunken state alerts Lorenzo and after an exchange of words, he threatens to have Stan arrested. Without thinking, Stan tells him that Diavolo will hear of this unless he leaves them alone. Ollie tries to make amends for Stan's outburst but completely blows their master's cover when he tells Lorenzo that Stan had really meant the Marquis de San Marco. With this the tavern is surrounded just as Diavolo has the petticoat in his grasp. After a brief skirmish he is captured by Lorenzo, who claims his prize and Zerlina's hand. Diavolo and the boys are sentenced to be shot and as the execution is about to take place, Stan asks for one last request - to blow his nose. He takes out his red handkerchief and in doing so enrages a nearby bull which scatters the firing squad. Diavolo makes his escape on horseback, closely followed by Stan and Ollie on the back of the bull.

Released in the US as **THE DEVIL'S BROTHER** and was based on Auber's 1830 comic opera *Fra Diavolo*, with Stan and Ollie portraying the re-written roles of Giacomo and Beppo. The film became one of their most loved pictures. Charley Rogers directed the scenes involving the boys, while Hal Roach took control over the rest of the movie. It contained several never-to-be-forgotten scenes, including Stan playing a game called "kneesie-earsie-nosie," where he slaps his knees then grabs his left ear with his right hand and his nose with his left, then reversing the action after every slap of the knee. This not only baffled Ollie and the innkeeper in the film, but cinema audiences as well.

Did You Know only a safety net prevented Ollie from falling to almost certain death while filming LIBERTY (1929). He had jumped down onto a "safety platform" to prove to Stan that it was safe!

What Was The Film When..?

ME AND MY PAL

Directed by **Charles Rogers & Lloyd French**, Produced by **Hal Roach**, Edited by **Bert Jordan**, Filmed - Mar 1933, Released - Apr 22, 1933 by MGM, Running time - 2 reels

With: **James Finlayson** (Mr. Peter Cucumber), **Nat Clifford** (Hives the butler and radio announcer's voice), **Eddie Dunn** (Cab driver), **James Morton, Charles McMurphy, Eddie Baker** (Policemen), **Bobby Dunn** (Telegram boy), **Charlie Hall** (Florist delivery man), **Marion Bardell** (Ollie's intended bride), **Carroll Borland, Mary Kornman** (Bridesmaids), **Charley Young** (Usher).

Ollie is about to marry the only daughter of rich oil magnate Mr. Peter Cucumber. Stan is the best man, and for once appears to have everything in hand. He gives Ollie his wedding present, a jigsaw puzzle, and starts to piece it together whilst waiting for the cab to arrive to take them to the wedding. Ollie pulls up a chair and joins in, and it isn't long before the cabby, a policeman (who has handed the cabby a parking ticket) and a telegram boy (who is delivering an important telegram) are all totally engrossed in the puzzle. Meanwhile the wedding party is awaiting Ollie's arrival. Mr. Cucumber's patience finally snaps with the arrival of Stan's wreath, instead of the flowers he should have ordered, and he storms round to Ollie's house to see what the delay is. It is discovered that the final piece of the jigsaw is missing, and the cop refuses to let anybody leave until it is found. He orders everyone in the room to be searched, but the cabby is not happy at being pushed around, and throws a punch at the officer, with the fight escalating into a free-for-all. A squad car arrives and all are arrested, apart from Stan, hiding under an upturned chair, and Ollie who has climbed the chimney. Stan then hands Ollie the telegram delivered earlier, which strongly advises him to sell his shares in The Great International Horsecollar Corporation, a move guaranteeing him a profit of $2 million. Ollie is just about to telephone, when a radio announcement informs him that the very shares in question have suffered a spectacular crash, thus losing him his fortune. Stan is about to leave, when he finds the final piece to the puzzle. He starts to piece it back together again, before Ollie throws him through the door and hurls the jigsaw around the room.

ME AND MY PAL was the only Laurel and Hardy short credited with two directors.

(Ollie) 'Well here's another nice bucket of suds you've gotten me into.' (*SAPS AT SEA*)

Any Nuts?

THE MIDNIGHT PATROL

Directed by **Lloyd French**, Produced by **Hal Roach**, Edited by **Bert Jordan**, Filmed - Jun/Jul 1933, Released - Aug 3, 1933 by MGM, Running time - 2 reels.

With: **Nat Clifford** (Safe-cracker), **Frank Brownlee** (Chief Brassbottom), **Eddie Dunn** (Sergeant), **Charlie Hall** (Trying to steal spare tyre), **Robert Kortman** (Hank, tyre-stealing accomplice), **James Morton, Edgar Dearing, Tiny Sandford** (Policemen), **Billy Bletcher** (Voice on patrol car radio), **Harry Bernard** (Man standing by cell).

For once Stan and Ollie are on the right side of the law, working as police officers together on their first day. During their lunch break they have a set-to with two hoods trying to steal the patrol car's spare tyre. The boys are then called to investigate a prowler at 24, Walnut Avenue, but their car fails to start, and during the distraction the address is forgotten. Stan goes to a nearby shop to phone the station, mistaking a safe-cracker as the shop owner. Between them they try to open the safe, before Ollie arrives on the scene and duly arrests the villain. The boys speed to the scene of the supposed break in (minus the tyres from the patrol car), and arrive just as the prowler is entering the house through the cellar. The boys follow, only to find the cellar door locked. They then use the top of a stone bench as a battering ram and smash down the front door, before crashing through the staircase, with their fall broken by a barrel of sauerkraut in the cellar. The intruder also falls through the hole left in the stairs, and after a struggle, is knocked unconscious and hauled off to the station. The boys, expecting a promotion for their good work, book the prowler for "robbing a house without a licence!" Unfortunately the prowler turns out to be Police Chief Brassbottom, who had been locked out of his own home. The boys realise the mistake and make a run for it as the chief draws a pistol and fires at them.

BUSY BODIES

Directed by **Lloyd French**, Produced by **Hal Roach**, Edited by **Bert Jordan**, Filmed - Jul 1933, Released - Oct 7, 1933 by MGM, Running time - 2 reels.

(Girlfriend) 'I just love soldiers.' (Ollie pointing to Stan) 'Meet the general.' (*MEN O' WAR*)

With: **Tiny Sandford** (Foreman), **Charlie Hall** (Aggrieved worker).

Also appeared: Jack Hill, Dick Gilbert, Charley Young.

It's a lovely sunny morning as Stan and Ollie drive to work at the timber yard, where they make even the easiest task seem difficult. Ollie starts work on a window frame, but traps his fingers. Efforts to free him prove unsuccessful, so Stan tries a more technical approach by consulting the blueprint, only this doesn't help matters as it's a print of the Boulder Dam! Stan climbs onto the workbench to get better leverage and sends the pair of them crashing into a fellow workman (Charlie Hall), who picks himself up and thumps Ollie before turning on Stan. Stan's intended "hay-maker" misses its mark and he slugs Ollie instead. This earns him the worker's instant friendship, so in return Stan offers his new buddy a cigar. He sits down to enjoy the smoke just as Stan beckons the foreman over pointing to the "No Smoking" sign on the wall. The culprit is thrown out of the shop and the boys get back to work. Stan then planes a piece out of Ollie's trousers, so is hit on the head with a large saw. Stan's retribution is to push a glue brush into his workmate's face. With the bristles well and truly stuck, Stan tries to make amends by shaving them off using a wood plane. When Ollie receives a soaking as well, he snatches at the hosepipe Stan is using, pulling the sink from the wall, which sends him tottering into a vertical pulley, and crashing through the floorboards into a sawdust vent. Stan rushes outside to see him stuck fast in the vent high up on the workshop wall. He fetches a ladder to try and rescue his pal, but back in the workshop, a barrel of shellac falls through the hole left in the floorboards and into the vent, smacking Ollie up the backside with such velocity, that it sends the pair of them falling backwards, still on the ladder, demolishing the foreman's office. The foreman clambers from the wreckage and gives chase, but the boys are saved when the barrel of shellac knocks him out. They leave in such a hurry that they drive their car through a large band saw, cutting it clean in half.

WILD POSES

Directed by **Robert McGowan**, Produced by **Robert McGowan for Hal Roach**, Edited by **William Terhune**, Filmed - Aug 1933, Released - Oct 28, 1933 by MGM, Running time - 2 reels.

(Commandant) 'Come come man, what is your number?' (Stan) 'Hollywood 4368.' (*BEAU HUNKS*)

Any Nuts?

With: **Spanky McFarland** (Baby at photographers), **Franklin Pangborn** (Otto Phocus), **Emerson Treacy** (Spanky's father, Emerson), **Gay Seabrook** (Spanky's mother, Gay), **"Stymie" Beard**, **Tommy Bond**, **Darby Billings**, **Jerry Tucker** (The Little Rascals).

Spanky McFarland's parents enter him in a baby photo contest, hoping to win the $100 first prize. When Spanky overhears the photographer, Otto Phocus, talking to his parents, he is reluctant to pose as he is led to believe the camera is going to chop off his nose and then shoot him! His father tries to reassure him by posing first, only to receive a jet of water in the face from the camera that has been sabotaged by the other contestants. They all sit for a family portrait, and this time it's Spanky's mother who gets a soaking. One hour later Otto finally takes Spanky's photo, but to no avail, as it's been ruined by the little rascals turning on the light in the dark room.

Stan and Ollie play a small part at the start of this Our Gang film. A salesman is trying to sell a mother the idea of having her two charming babies photographed. The two in question are the boys squabbling over a large bottle of milk.

DIRTY WORK

Directed by **Lloyd French**, Produced by **Hal Roach**, Edited by **Bert Jordan**, Filmed - Aug 1933, Released - Nov 25, 1933 by MGM, Running time - 2 reels.

With: **Lucien Littlefield** (Professor Noodle), **Sam Adams** (Jessup the butler).

Also appeared: Jiggs the chimpanzee.

As chimney sweeps, the boys make the unfortunate mistake of calling at the house of Professor Noodle, a mad scientist who has been working on a rejuvenation formula for over twenty years. After several mishaps whilst trying to clean the chimney, Ollie climbs onto the roof to supervise the sweeping. Even there he isn't safe from Stan, who nearly blows his head off

---

(Stan) 'They took me to the hospital.' (Ollie) 'Was it serious?' (Stan) 'Yes, the doctor says I might get hydrophosphates.' *(HELPMATES)*

when he replaces a broken brush extension with a loaded gun, and then rams it up the chimney. A tug-of-war with the brush ensues, and Ollie is dragged down the chimney, closely followed by the stack which comes down on top of him. With the room now well and truly covered in soot, they set about cleaning up the mess, with Stan shovelling more of the soot down the front of Ollie's trousers, than into the sack he is holding. Suddenly the professor bursts into the room declaring his "elixir of life" a success, having changed a duck back into a duckling. The boys witness him change the duckling into an egg with just a few drops of the formula. The professor then goes off to find his butler, so he can carry out a human experiment. Stan and Ollie decide to try out the formula for themselves, and place a large fish in the water tank. Ollie is about to administer a small dose, when Stan accidentally tips him in, along with all the remaining formula. He emerges seconds later from the bubbling foam filled water as a chimpanzee and replies to a tearful Stan *'I have nothing to say!*

SONS OF THE DESERT

Directed by **William Seiter**, Produced by **Hal Roach**, Edited by **Bert Jordan**, Filmed - Oct 1933, Released - Dec 29, 1933 by MGM, Running time - 68 minutes.

With: **Mae Busch** (Mrs Lottie Hardy), **Dorothy Christy** (Mrs Betty Laurel), **John Elliott** ("Exhausted" ruler), **Charley Chase** (Mrs Hardy's brother, Charley), **Lucien Littlefield** (Dr. Horace Meddick), **Harry Bernard** (Policeman), **Sam Lufkin**, **Charlie Hall** (Waiters), **Ty Parvis** (Singer at convention), **Billy Gilbert** (Voice-over for Mr. Ruttledge).

Also appeared: Charley Young, William Gillespie, Eddie Baker, Jimmy Aubrey, Chet Brandenberg, Max Wagner, Ernie Alexander, Baldwin Cooke, Stanley Blystone, Pat Harmon, Bobby Burns, The Hollywood American Legion Post.

Stan and Ollie are sworn to attend their fraternity's 87th annual convention of the Sons Of The Desert in Chicago. Ollie's wife however has organised a trip into the mountains and forbids him to go. Ollie feigns illness while Stan fixes it with a doctor to

Any Nuts?

prescribe an ocean voyage, knowing full well that Mrs Hardy is a very bad sailor. The doctor in fact turns out to be a veterinarian, who describes Ollie's condition as "Canus Delirus" and prescribes a voyage to Honolulu as the only cure. The boys head off to Chicago for the convention, with their wives thinking they are aboard ship bound for Honolulu. The boys have a great time at the bash where they unwittingly team up with Mrs Hardy's effervescent long lost brother Charley, not knowing that the Honolulu liner, S S *Muana*, is foundering in a storm at sea. Their wives hear about the disaster and rush to the steamship company to be told that the survivors will arrive next day. Meanwhile the boys have returned home and find out about the sinking, so decide to stay up in the attic for the night, intending to go down in the morning and tell of their supposed ordeal. Their grief stricken wives go to the movies to try and take their minds off the tragedy, only to spot the boys cavorting on a news reel of the convention. They return home and search the attic, so Stan and Ollie climb onto the roof in the pouring rain, but are collared by a cop as they shin down the drainpipe. They are escorted to the door where they spin a fantastic yarn to their wives about the sinking, that is until Mrs Hardy tells them that the rescue ship doesn't actually arrive in port until the next day. The boys then dig an even deeper hole for themselves by saying they "shiphiked" their way home. Mrs Hardy asks Ollie to tell her the truth, but he sticks firmly to the story. Stan though is not so strong and breaks down and confesses all when his wife asks him the same question. The Laurels return home where Stan is pampered by his loving wife, his reward for telling the truth, while in the Hardy household, Ollie has everything bar the kitchen sink hurled at him.

Stan and Ollie's friendly poke of the finger at the American lodge set-up. Released in Britain under the working title FRATERNALLY YOURS, it was one of Stan and Ollie's biggest box office hits as well as one of the top grossing films of 1934. The film title is used today all over the world and relates to members belonging to the Laurel and Hardy Appreciation Society. "Sons of the Desert" can currently be found in the USA, Australasia, Belgium, Denmark, Great Britain, France, Germany, Holland, Italy, Norway and Switzerland and continues to flourish. Each fan club is called a "tent" and is named after a Laurel and Hardy film (Come Clean Tent, Blotto Tent etc.), meeting regularly to watch the boys' films and attend Laurel and Hardy related events (see "Sons" constitution at back of book).

(Ollie) 'Don't you realize that I'm about to become a big oil magnate? You know what a magnate is don't you?' (Stan) 'Sure, a thing that eats cheese.' (*ME AND MY PAL*)

What Was The Film When..?

HOLLYWOOD PARTY

No director credited, Produced by **Harry Rapf & Howard Dietz**, Edited by **George Boemier**, Filmed - Mar 1933 - Mar 1934, Released - Jun 1, 1934 by MGM, Running time - 68 minutes.

With: **Jimmy Durante** (As himself /Schnarzan), **Jean Durante** (As herself), **Lupe Velez** (Angry lady at bar), **Tom Kennedy** (Doorman, Beavers), **Richard Carle** (Schnarzan's manager, Knapp), **George Givot** (Liondora), **Edwin Maxwell** (Liondora's manager, Buddy Goldfard), **Jack Pearl** (Baron Munchausen), **Tom Herbert** (Bar attendant).

Also appeared: Ted Healy, The Three Stooges, Robert Young, Eddie Quillan, Rychard Cramer, Baldwin Cooke, Polly Moran, Charles Butterworth, June Clyde, Tom London, Ben Bard, Frank Austin (Voice-overs supplied by Walt Disney and Billy Bletcher).

The popularity of Schnarzan the jungle film star is waning due to the fact that the lions in his films are too tame. A big game hunter, Baron Munchausen, returns from Africa with some new lions which Schnarzan hopes to acquire, with Liondora, a film rival, also wanting to use them in his own films. In an attempt to obtain the animals, Schnarzan throws a lavish Hollywood party where he hopes to persuade the Baron to sell them to him. Stan and Ollie, the original vendors, turn up at the party intent on confronting the Baron, as they are having difficulty in cashing his cheque for 50,000 tiddlywinks. After a set-to with an aggressive doorman, the boys' search takes them to the bar, where they battle it out with a hot tempered lady guest, using eggs as the ammunition. The doorman and the rest of the staff chase Stan and Ollie outside where the boys let the lions loose, causing the party guests to flee.

Following the success of THE HOLLYWOOD REVUE OF 1929, MGM used the formula again for a revue of 1933. Due to a shortage of stars appearing (Clark Gable, Joan Crawford and Johnny Weissmuller were just a few stars who were originally to appear) directors coming and going (Russell Mack, Richard Boleslawski, George Stevens and Charles Riesner) and a filming schedule that lasted twelve months, the picture was labelled a flop. Stan and Ollie who had joined the cast in September, received the plaudits for saving the picture from being a total disaster.

Any Nuts?

OLIVER THE EIGHTH

Directed by **Lloyd French**, Produced by **Hal Roach**, Edited by **Bert Jordan**, Filmed - Dec 1933/Jan 1934, Released - Feb 1934 by MGM, Running time - 3 reels.

With: **Mae Busch** (Wealthy widow), **Jack Barty** (Jitters the butler).

Stan and Ollie run a barber's shop, and when they spot a newspaper advert regarding a wealthy widow seeking a new husband, they both decide to apply. With both letters written, Ollie posts his own but hides Stan's in the shop. Ollie soon receives a reply stating that he has been chosen to be the lady's new partner. He leaves the shop in Stan's less-than-capable hands while he heads off for a life of luxury. When Stan finds his letter, he swaps the shop for a dubious looking gold brick and a hand full of nuts, before storming round to the lady's house demanding his "cut." Dinner is served, with the boys enduring a make believe meal involving imaginary soup and wine. They are summoned away from the table by the cranky butler, who informs Ollie that later that night he will have his throat cut by his mistress, as she was once jilted by an Oliver on the eve of her wedding day. Since then seven other Olivers have crossed her path and all suffered the same fate - with Ollie set to become Oliver the eighth! With the doors locked and the windows barred, the boys retire to bed. They decide to take it in turns to stay awake, yet come Stan's turn he dozes off almost immediately, his excuse being that he was dreaming he was awake and then woke to find himself asleep! Ollie suspends a brick above Stan's head to keep his mind occupied. However the plan backfires when Ollie is knocked cold by the brick, just as the widow enters the room sharpening her knife. He is about to become another victim when he wakes up screaming in the barber's chair as Stan is about to shave him. Luckily, he was only dreaming.

A similar dream sequence ending as used in THE LAUREL - HARDY MURDER CASE. Released in Britain as THE PRIVATE LIFE OF OLIVER THE EIGHTH.

Mae Busch
1891 - 1946

Any Nuts ?

GOING BYE-BYE!   8

Directed by **Charles Rogers**, Produced by **Hal Roach**, Edited by **Bert Jordan**, Filmed - May 1934, Released - Jun 23, 1934 by MGM, Running time - 2 reels.

With: **Walter Long** (Butch Long), **Mae Busch** (Butch's girlfriend, Mae), **Harry Dunkinson** (Judge), **Baldwin Cooke** (Policeman in court), **Ellinor Vanderveer** (Juror), **Sam Lufkin** (Man with advice).

Also appeared: Fred Holmes, Lester Dorr, Charles Dorety.

As key witnesses at a trial, Stan and Ollie's evidence puts Butch Long behind bars for the rest of his life. Stan further infuriates the criminal when, disappointed by the sentence, he asks the judge why the prisoner isn't being hanged! Butch swears revenge, promising them he'll break off their legs and wrap them around their necks if he ever catches up with them again. Outside court, a man (Sam Lufkin) advises the boys to get out of town as Butch never forgets. They decide to take the advice, and advertise for a third person to travel east with them, to share the driving and expenses. A lady telephones about the trip, requesting they leave right away. Meanwhile, Butch has jumped train on the way to prison and returns to his girlfriend's apartment, the very lady accompanying the boys on their trip. Stan and Ollie arrive, and Butch thinking it's the cops, hides in a trunk. The lady asks if she can bring along a friend, explaining that he has managed to lock himself inside a trunk. With Butch almost suffocating, Stan tries to help the situation by opening the apartment window! The boys bore holes in the trunk and then try to melt off the lock with a blowtorch, succeeding only in setting the trunk on fire. Butch then nearly drowns when they put out the flames with the fire hose, and eventually breaks free. He chases the boys into another room just as the police arrive. Butch is re-arrested, but not in time to save the boys from his sworn revenge.

THEM THAR HILLS   9

Directed by **Charles Rogers**, Produced by **Hal Roach**, Edited by **Bert Jordan**, Filmed - Jun 1934, Released - Jul 21, 1934 by MGM, Running time - 2 reels.

(Ollie) 'You are upset, aren't you?' (Stan) 'Upset? I'm housebroken.' *(BABES IN TOYLAND)*

What Was The Film When...?

With: **Charlie Hall** (Mr. Hall), **Mae Busch** (Mrs Hall), **Billy Gilbert** (Doctor), **Bobby Dunn**, **Sam Lufkin**, **Dick Alexander** ("Moonshiners"), **Eddie Baker**, **Baldwin Cooke**, **Bobby Burns** (Policemen).

Ollie has a gout-ridden foot due to too much good living, and is advised by his doctor to take a trip into the mountains, and drink plenty of the mountain water. The boys hire a trailer and find a perfect spot next to an old well, where moments earlier, a gang of "moonshiners" had poured their illicit hooch following a shoot-out with the cops. The boys prepare dinner with beans and coffee on the menu, but when Stan fetches water from the well they notice it has a peculiar colour. Ollie explains that it's the iron in it, and that's why the doctor told them to drink plenty. The "water" soon takes effect and it isn't long before the boys are quite drunk. A Mr. and Mrs Hall call, after running out of gas further up the trail. Mr. Hall returns to his car with a spare can, while his wife stays for some supper and a few cups of "water". Her husband returns to find all three hopelessly drunk and singing bawdily to the tune of *The Old Spinning Wheel*. He shows his displeasure and is soon involved in an altercation with the boys. With a plate of butter on top of his head and a plunger stuck to his forehead, Mr. Hall unhooks the trailer from the car, tipping it up and sending the boys crashing through the side. Their reply is to cover him from head to foot in molasses and feathers. In turn Ollie has his pants set on fire, and when he jumps into the well to douse the flames, it explodes sending him sky high.

Charlie Hall proved to be the perfect foil for Stan and Ollie. His short fuse temper was illustrated to the full in THEM THAR HILLS and again in the sequel TIT FOR TAT. Like Stan he was of English stock, born in Birmingham, August 19, 1899. In 1915 he left for America where he worked for Mack Sennett and Joe Rock. Amongst his early films was NEAR DUBLIN made in 1923 starring Stan and James Finlayson. In 1927 he appeared in his first Laurel and Hardy film, LOVE 'EM AND WEEP, one of 47 appearances he would make. His early claim to fame was the instigator of the massive pie fight in THE BATTLE OF THE CENTURY. He made his final appearance with the boys in 1940 before moving on to appear in other comedies, including working with Abbott and Costello.

(Stan) 'Why don't you draw the money out of the bank, pay off the furniture and own it outright? You wouldn't have any interest to pay and you wouldn't have any hounds in your fireplace.' *(THICKER THAN WATER)*

BABES IN TOYLAND

Directed by **Charles Rogers & Gus Meins**, Produced by **Hal Roach**, Edited by **William Terhune & Bert Jordan**, Filmed - Aug-Oct 1934, Released - Nov 30, 1934 by MGM, Running time - 79 minutes.

With: **Henry Brandon** (Silas Barnaby), **Charlotte Henry** (Little Bo Peep), **Felix Knight** (Tom Tom), **Florence Roberts** (Mother Peep), **Virginia Karns** (Mother Goose), **Tiny Sandford, Eddie Baker** (Ducking stool operators), **Kewpie Morgan** (Old King Cole), **Alice Moore** (Queen of Hearts), **Billy Bletcher** (Chief of police), **Sumner Getchell** (Tom Thumb), **John George** (Barnaby's side-kick), **Alice Dahl** (Little Miss Muffet), **Johnny Downs** (Little Boy Blue), **William Burress** (Toymaker), **Ferdinand Munier** (Santa Claus), **Frank Austin** (Justice of the peace), **Pete Gordon** (The cat), **Angelo Rossito** (Elmer the pig), **Alice Cooke** (Old Mother Hubbard).

Also appeared: Jean Darling, Marie Wilson, Gus Leonard, Charlie Hall, Baldwin Cooke, Jack Hill, Sam Lufkin, Fred Holmes, Payne Johnson, Charley Rogers, Our Gang Kids.

Ollie Dee and Stannie Dum live in Toyland, lodging with Mother Peep. Silas Barnaby, Toyland's meanest resident, asks Mother Peep's daughter Bo to marry him, but when he is turned down because she loves Tom Tom, he threatens to throw her mother onto the street as she cannot pay her mortgage. Stan and Ollie tell her not to worry, promising to borrow the money from their boss the toymaker. They arrive for work at the toy factory as Santa Claus calls for his order of toy soldiers. It is discovered that Stan has mixed up the order, and instead of making 600 soldiers one foot high, they have made 100 soldiers six feet high! When one of the soldiers wrecks the factory the boys are sacked. Barnaby calls for the mortgage and tries to bribe Bo into accepting his proposal, agreeing to hand over the mortgage papers as a wedding present if she accepts. The boys try to steal the papers, but are caught and sentenced to banishment in Bogeyland by Old King Cole. Fortunately for them, Bo reluctantly agrees to the wedding and they are reprieved. On the wedding day Ollie leads the veiled bride to Barnaby's house for the ceremony, and with the vows

What Was The Film When..?

(Top) At war again with Charlie Hall in THEM THAR HILLS and below, Ollie in trustful mood in OLIVER THE EIGHTH

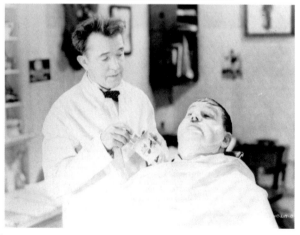

Any Nuts ?

(Top) Stan's sister and Fanny Laurel in TWICE TWO, and below the boys are no match for Lupe Velez in THE HOLLYWOOD PARTY

SONS OF THE DESERT wives Dorothy Christy (Betty Laurel) and Mae Busch (Lottie Hardy) in one of Laurel and Hardy's most popular and loved films

Any Nuts ?

Officers Laurel and Hardy at work together in
THE MIDNIGHT PATROL

What Was The Film When..?

exchanged, reminds Barnaby of his agreement. The papers are duly handed over, and Ollie tears them up. Barnaby then lifts the veil to kiss his new wife, only to discover he has been tricked and "married" Stan instead! With Bo back in Tom Tom's arms Toyland rejoices, but unknown to the happy couple, Barnaby is already planning his revenge. He steals Elmer, one of The Three Little Pigs, and gets one of his henchmen to plant some sausages, along with Elmer's hat and violin, in Tom Tom's house. He is arrested and charged with "pignapping" and sent to Bogeyland as punishment, yet when Stan and Ollie later search Barnaby's house, they find Elmer safe in the cellar. Old King Cole offers a 50,000 guinea reward for the capture of Barnaby, who has escaped down the wishing well to Bogeyland, with Stan and Ollie in hot pursuit. Meanwhile, Bo has also entered the sinister world looking for Tom Tom. Barnaby finds the pair fast asleep, and when he summons his army of demons, the bogeymen, Bo, Tom Tom and the boys flee. They all return safely to Toyland where Stan and Ollie are hailed as heroes, but the rejoicing is cut short when Barnaby and his army storm the Toyland gates. The boys take shelter in the toy warehouse, where Stan hits upon the idea of using the 100 giant soldiers to fight off the intruders. In unison the soldiers march out of the warehouse to confront Barnaby and his demons, forcing them to retreat back through the Toyland gates.

"And they all lived happily ever afterward."

Based very loosely on Victor Herbert's 1903 fairy-tale operetta of the same name. It proved to be Laurel and Hardy's most elaborate and extravagant venture, with the town of Toyland created at enormous expense. There were small roles in the film for Stan's old associates from The Stan Jefferson Trio, Baldwin and Alice Cooke. The film is probably better known today under its re-issue title MARCH OF THE WOODEN SOLDIERS.

THE LIVE GHOST

Directed by **Charles Rogers**, Produced by **Hal Roach**, Edited by **Louis MacManus**, Filmed - Nov 1934, Released - Dec 8, 1934 by MGM, Running time - 2 reels.

Any Nuts?

With: **Walter Long** (Salty sea captain), **Arthur Housman** (Drunk cabin mate), **Charlie Hall** (Sailor in saloon), **Leo Willis** (Sailor's pal), **Mae Busch** (Drunkard's wife), **Harry Bernard** (Bartender).

Also appeared: Pete Gordon, Charlie Sullivan, Jack Lipson, Dick Gilbert, Baldwin Cooke, Sam Lufkin, Arthur Rowlands, Hubert Diltz, Bill Moore, John Power.

A burly sea captain has difficulty in obtaining a crew as his ship is rumoured to be haunted. He approaches Stan and Ollie, fishing on the quayside on their day off from the fish market, who agree to help him shanghai a crew for a dollar a head. Stan enters the local saloon armed with a bag of eggs. He sits down with the sailors and bets one of them (Leo Willis) that he can't put an egg in his mouth without breaking it. The sailor easily wins the wager until Stan socks him under the chin. Stan is chased outside where Ollie smacks the sailor over the head with a frying pan. The trick proves successful a number of times before the boys swap roles. With Stan now wielding the pan, he not only knocks out Ollie and the chasing sailor, but is knocked cold himself when he tries it on with the captain. The boys find themselves at sea along with the crew they helped shanghai. They are saved from a lynching by the captain who promises them protection while aboard ship. He also has a stern warning for the crew, that if the word "ghost" is even muttered, he will turn the culprit's head so that *'when he's walking North, he'll be looking South.'* Some ten ports later the crew goes ashore. As usual the boys stay aboard along with their drunken cabin mate who has been forbidden to leave the boat. Nevertheless he disobeys the captain's orders and sneaks off after placing a suitcase under his bedclothes. Whilst the boys are preparing for bed, Stan finds a pistol under a pillow, and when it accidentally goes off, thinks he has shot dead their cabin mate. They search below for a body bag as the drunk returns to his bed after falling into a trough of whitewash. The boys return and put him in the bag and throw him overboard. He climbs back on deck, still covered in whitewash, scaring Stan and Ollie witless. The captain returns to the ship with a girlfriend (Mae Busch) who is in fact the drunk's estranged wife. The boys tell the captain about their run in with the "ghost," at which point he administers the punishment promised and twists their heads around the wrong way.

(Stan) 'After you're gone, do you want to be buried or shall I have you stuffed?' (Ollie) 'Why I think that I'd rather...what do you mean stuffed?' (Stan) 'Well I thought it'd be nice to keep you in the living room.' *(FRA DIAVOLO)*

What Was The Film When..?

Arthur Housman
1890 - 1942

TIT FOR TAT

Directed by **Charles Rogers**, Produced by **Hal Roach**, Edited by **Bert Jordan**, Filmed - Dec 1934, Released - Jan 5, 1935 by MGM, Running time - 2 reels.

With: **Charlie Hall** (Mr. Hall), **Mae Busch** (Mrs Hall), **James Morton** (Policeman), **Bobby Dunn** (Shoplifter).

Also appeared: Baldwin Cooke, Jack Hill, Pete Gordon, Elsie MacKaye, Dick Gilbert, Lester Dorr, Viola Richard.

Stan and Ollie are the proprietors of a newly opened electrical store, opening a day late due to Stan's nervous breakdown. They go next door to introduce themselves to a Mr. and Mrs Hall who run the grocery shop. The couple turn out to be the very folks they had met during a previous trip into the mountains (See THEM THAR HILLS). The boys receive a less than warm welcome from Mr. Hall, and are ordered out of the store. Later, whilst up a ladder attending to the shop sign, Ollie has to contend with Stan's antics involving the shop's elevator and finds himself stranded on Mrs Hall's bedroom window ledge. When Ollie and Mrs Hall come down the stairs together, her husband accuses him of having designs on his wife, and warns him to stay clear, or he'll hit him so hard that Stan will feel it! With Ollie's reputation now in tatters, he demands an apology. The row escalates into a tit-for-tat wrecking spree, with both shops bearing the full brunt. Just as things are getting totally out of hand, a policeman steps in to calm the quarrel, and find out the reason for the argument. Ollie pleads his innocence, and Mr. Hall is made to apologise. The pair shake hands and the boys return to their shop to find it entirely stripped of its contents, having been visited several times during the day by a shoplifter.

This was the only Laurel and Hardy sequel, with the boys carrying on their conflict with Charlie Hall from THEM THAR HILLS. It was nominated for Best Live Action Short Subject in the 1936 Oscars, where it was placed second.

What Was The Film When..?

THE FIXER-UPPERS

Directed by **Charles Rogers**, Produced by **Hal Roach**, Edited by **Bert Jordan**, Filmed - Jan 1935, Released - Feb 9, 1935 by MGM, Running time - 2 reels.

With: **Mae Busch** (Pierre's wife), **Charles Middleton** (Pierre Gustave), **Arthur Housman** (Drunkard), **Noah Young** (Bartender), **James Morton**, **Dick Gilbert**, **Jack Hill** (Policemen), **Bob O'Conor** (Waiter), **Bobby Dunn** (Passerby in hall).

It's the middle of winter in Paris and the boys are trying to earn a living selling greetings cards, with Ollie the card designer and Stan the verse writer. They call on one unhappy lady (Mae Busch), who fears she has lost her husband's affections, as he is totally wrapped up in his work as an artist. Stan comes up with an idea for her to win back her husband's love. He tells her he once knew a lady in a similar predicament, who hired a fellow to make love to her in front of her husband, who feeling jealous, realises his love for her. The lover was paid a large amount of money for arousing the husband's lost affections and they all lived happily ever after. Thinking this is a splendid idea she offers to pay Ollie $50 for his services as her "lover" for the day. After Ollie is assured of the happy ending, he agrees and is in the middle of a long passionate embrace when her husband, Pierre, walks in on them. Unfortunately the plan doesn't quite go to script, with Pierre admitting his jealousy but ordering Ollie to return at midnight for a duel to the death. His wife begs him to reconsider but Pierre, reputed to be the best shot in all of Paris, will have none of it. As is the custom, the two swap business cards and the boys leave. They spend the afternoon in a bar, as Ollie ponders his fate over a last beer. Stan persuades him not to show up, claiming that Pierre's threat to track him all over the world if he doesn't show, is just a load of baloney. Ollie rings Pierre up and gives him a piece of his mind, infuriating him so much, he storms out of the apartment swearing to kill Ollie on the spot. A drunk enters the bar but is refused service, so the boys order for him and in return he buys all their cards. Hours later the boys are so sozzled they pass out. The police arrive and take them back to the address found in Ollie's possession, printed on Pierre's business card!! They are put to bed as Pierre returns home.

Did You Know despite Stan's association with Charlie Chaplin during their Fred Karno Days, he was not mentioned in the book Charlie Chaplin, My Autobiography, even though a photo of the pair appears in the publication.

His wife explains the earlier misunderstanding and the pair swear their undying love, until the romantic interlude is interrupted by Stan's snoring. Pierre finds the boys in his wife's bed and the reconciliation is forgotten. With pistols drawn, Ollie puts on an act of bravado after the lady tells him she has swapped the bullets for blanks. She tells him to feign death when fired at, then make his escape when her husband flees from the supposed "murder." The plan works a treat, until Pierre wants to cut up the "body." Ollie jumps up and the boys escape after he crashes through the door. Pierre gives chase into the snowy streets, but Ollie evades capture by hiding in a dustbin, which is emptied onto a garbage truck.

The storyline for the film was based on the 1927 silent SLIPPING WIVES, with Ollie this time swapping roles with Stan to become the pretend lover.

BONNIE SCOTLAND

Directed by **James Horne**, Produced by **Hal Roach**, Edited by **Bert Jordan**, Filmed - May/Jun 1935, Released - Aug 23, 1935 by MGM, Running time - 80 minutes.

With: **June Lang** (Lorna McLaurel), **William Janney** (Alan Douglas), **Vernon Steele** (Colonel Gregor McGregor), **Anne Grey** (Lady Violet Ormsby), **James Finlayson** (Sergeant Finlayson), **Lionel Belmore** (Blacksmith), **Dick Wessell** (Blacksmith's assistant), **Maurice Black** (Khan Mir Jutra), **James Mack** (Butler), **James May** (Postman), **Brandon Hurst** (Military policeman), **Mary Gordon** (Hotel proprietor, Mrs Bickerdyke), **Daphne Pollard** (Millie the maid), **David Torrence** (Attorney, Mr. Miggs), **Claude King** (General Fletcher), **Marvin Hatley** (Soldier with accordion).

Also appeared: May Beatty, Jack Hill, Noah Young, Dan Maxwell, Frank Benson, Charlie Hall, Bob O'Conor, Leo Willis, Sam Lufkin, Bobby Dunn, John Sutherland's Scotch Pipers.

Despite having only a week of their jail sentence to serve, Stan persuades Ollie to escape so he can be present at the reading of the will of his late grandfather, Angus Ian McLaurel. They stow away on a cattle boat, arriving in Scotland expecting to inherit the McLaurel estate, one of the richest in Scotland. This however is bequeathed to Lorna McLaurel on condition that she lives with her appointed guardian Colonel Gregor McGregor, until she reaches her 21st birthday. As the colonel is stationed in India, this means leaving behind her beloved Scotland and sweetheart Alan Douglas. Despite their high hopes, Stan and Ollie's inheritance amounts to a set of bagpipes - apparently blown at Waterloo, and a snuff box. The boys suffer a further setback when they are thrown out of their hotel room after setting the bed on fire while trying to cook a fish for their dinner. Left penniless and in Ollie's case trouserless, they hear about a tailor's shop offer of a made-to-measure suit on a thirty day trial. They go to take up the offer but enter the wrong shop and sign up for the army, to be stationed in Pellore, India, at the very camp commanded by Colonel McGregor. Lorna's broken hearted sweetheart hears of the posting, so quits his job and joins up too, so he can be with Lorna again. In India, Lorna has settled down to her new life, unaware that the colonel's scheming sister, Lady Ormsby, has thrown all of Alan's love letters on the fire and is plotting to marry her off to her brother. Thinking that Alan has forgotten her, Lorna accepts Colonel McGregor's proposal, just as Alan and the boys arrive at camp. She soon finds out the truth when the maid of the house (who has been sacked by the colonel's sister for entertaining Sergeant Finlayson) shows her the love letters she has salvaged from the fire. Alan and the boys are sent as re-inforcements to a Scottish outpost that is under the threat of attack from Khan Mir Jutra and his followers, who intend to storm the fort after first luring the officers away to the palace. Colonel McGregor learns of the plan from a captured spy and sends Stan, Ollie, Alan and Sergeant Finlayson to the palace posing as officers, as Lorna arrives at the post searching for her sweetheart. Khan Mir Jutra realises he has been hoodwinked by his guests when he learns that the attack on the outpost was a failure and that all his men have been captured. The boys are chased into the palace gardens where they upset a number of bee hives, causing mayhem amongst both natives and the Scottish regiment marching towards the palace.

Some have stated that the film was a possible sequel to PARDON US as they have the same prison numbers (Stan 44634 and Ollie 44633) in both pictures. Working titles for the film included KILTS, McLAUREL AND McHARDY and LAUREL AND HARDY OF INDIA. The main plot of the picture concentrates on lovers Alan and Lorna's struggle to be reunited, but surprisingly ends with the

Any Nuts ?

question of the reconciliation unresolved. One delightful part of the film sees Stan marching out of step, rectifying his mistake by getting the rest of the regiment including Sergeant Finlayson to follow suit. The Scottish village seen at the beginning of the film was loaned to Roach by RKO, who had constructed it for the Katherine Hepburn film THE LITTLE MINISTER.

THICKER THAN WATER

Directed by **James Horne**, Produced by **Hal Roach**, Edited by **Ray Snyder**, Filmed - Jul 1935, Released - circa Aug 1935 by MGM, Running time - 2 reels.

With: **Daphne Pollard** (Mrs Hardy), **James Finlayson** (Mr. Finlayson/Auction owner), **Gladys Gale** (Lady bidding at auction), **Harry Bowen** (Auctioneer), **Charlie Hall, Ed Brandenberg** (Bank clerks), **Allen Cavan** (Doctor Allen), **Grace Goodall, Bess Flowers** (Nurses).

Also appeared: Lester Dorr, Baldwin Cooke.

Stan is lodging with the Hardys. After a disagreement over a furniture payment Ollie hasn't made, Stan urges him to put his foot down with his bossy wife and draw out their life savings of $300 to pay off the debt. Ollie thinks this is a splendid idea, but Mrs Hardy is adamant that the money stays in the bank. With further prompting from Stan, Ollie decides to go ahead with Stan's brainwave to teach his high and mighty wife a lesson. With the account closed, the boys go off to pay the loan, but call in on an auction on the way. They sit next to a lady who has set her heart on an antique grandfather clock. The lady then realises that she has left her money at home so asks Ollie to continue the bidding on her behalf until she returns with the cash. The price soon rises, especially with Stan bidding against his pal. With the price at $290, the clock is sold to Ollie who is made to pay for it by the auction room boss (James Finlayson), as the auction is about to close. The boys are carrying the clock home, when they stop for a rest whilst crossing the street, only to see the antique smashed to pieces by an oncoming truck. They arrive home, unaware that Mrs Hardy is wise to the bank withdrawal and the purchase at the auction. She hits Ollie with a frying pan so hard, that

(Ollie) 'Why did you get a vetarnarian?' (Stan) 'Well I didn't think his religion would make any difference.' *(SONS OF THE DESERT)*

he is rushed to hospital. When he has a relapse, Stan is called upon to be a blood donor but the transfusion goes wrong and has to be reversed. With their blood now well and truly mixed they leave hospital, each having inherited the other's looks and mannerisms.

Due to the movie industry's demand for feature length films, THICKER THAN WATER marked the end of an era, when it became Stan and Ollie's final regular short film.

THE BOHEMIAN GIRL

Directed by **James Horne & Charles Rogers**, Produced by **Hal Roach**, Edited by **Bert Jordan & Louis McManus**, Filmed - Oct 1935 - Jan 1936, Released - Feb 14, 1936 by MGM, Running time - 70 minutes.

With: **Mae Busch** (Ollie's wife), **Antonio Moreno** (Devilshoof), **Darla Hood** (Arline as a child), **Jacqueline Wells** (Arline), **William P. Carlton** (Count Arnheim), **James Finlayson** (Captain of the guard), **Zeffie Tilbury** (Gypsy Queen), **Harry Bernard** (Town crier), **James Morton** (Policeman), **Eddie Borden** (Robbed gent), **Harry Bowen** (Drunkard), **Bob O'Conor** (Waiter at tavern), **Bobby Dunn** (Cross-eyed barman), **Sam Lufkin** (Pickpocket victim poked in the eye), **Charlie Hall** (Voice-over for gypsy).

Also appeared: Thelma Todd, Felix Knight, Dick Gilbert, Leo Willis, Baldwin Cooke, Jack Hill, Mitchell Lewis, Margaret Mann, Alice Cooke, Laughing Gravy the dog, Yogi the myna bird.

The boys are members of a band of gypsies who set up camp in woods belonging to Count Arnheim. With a mutual hatred for each other, the Count orders the gypsies off his land, commanding his soldiers to flog anyone found trespassing on the estate. Night falls and the gypsies go into town to earn their living by pick-pocketing. Devilshoof, the secret lover of Ollie's wife, is caught in the castle grounds and is given a severe flogging. The band moves on, but as Ollie's wife tends her lover's wounds, she spots the Count's only child, Arline, searching for her pet rabbit, and takes revenge for the beating by kidnapping her. With the gypsies at their new camp, the child is introduced to Ollie as his

A publicity still from BONNIE SCOTLAND

(Top) Ollie Dee and Stannie Dum in one of their most lavishly produced films BABES IN TOYLAND, and below Lola Marcel (Sharon Lynne) gets the better of Stan in WAY OUT WEST

Any Nuts?

(Top) Charlie Hall (left) and Leo Willis about to fall foul of Stan's wager in THE LIVE GHOST, and below, sea captain Walter Long has three more for the "ghost ship".

What Was The Film When..?

Stan and Ollie feel the wrath of Daphne Pollard in **THICKER THAN WATER**

Any Nuts ?

own daughter. It isn't long before he and Stan are left to bring up the child alone, as his wife leaves with her lover, taking all the boys' valuables with them. Twelve years pass before the gypsies return again to the woods belonging to the Count, who is still mourning the loss of his daughter. With Ollie in town and Stan bottling wine, Arline becomes enchanted by the castle and wanders into the grounds where she is arrested. Ollie witnesses this and along with Stan, who has drank more wine than he has bottled, they try to rescue her, but are captured and sent to the torture chamber. As Arline is about to be flogged, her necklace, given to her as a child by the Count, is flung to the floor. The Count, there to witness the punishment, recognises the family heirloom and realises that he has found his long lost daughter. Happily re-united, Arline pleads with her father for the boys' release. Unfortunately her pleas come too late and Ollie emerges from his ordeal stretched to the height of a giant while Stan walks out squashed to the size of a midget.

Based on Michael Balfe's opera of 1843 and well remembered for Stan's hilarious attempts to bottle wine. Just days after the film was previewed however, Thelma Todd aged only thirty, was found dead behind the wheel of her car. A former beauty queen, she had appeared in several notable roles in Laurel and Hardy films, including Lady Plumtree in ANOTHER FINE MESS, and as Mrs Kennedy in UNACCUSTOMED AS WE ARE. Mystery surrounds the events to this day and although the death certificate stated carbon monoxide poisoning as cause of death, it provoked the question of was it suicide or murder due to Thelma's association with mobster Lucky Luciano? To save the film from receiving any bad publicity, the script was changed, and re-takes arranged the Gypsy Queen, whom Thelma had originally been cast to play, was now played by Zeffie Tilbury.

OUR RELATIONS

Directed by **Harry Lachman**, Produced by **Stan Laurel for Hal Roach**, Edited by **Bert Jordan**, Filmed - Mar-May 1936, Released - Oct 30, 1936 by MGM, Running time - 74 minutes.

With: **Daphne Pollard** (Mrs Hardy), **Betty Healy** (Mrs Laurel), **Sidney**

What Was The Film When..?

Toler (Captain), **Alan Hale** (Groagan the waiter), **Iris Adrian** (Alice, floozy at Denker's), **Lona Andre** (Lily, Alice's girlfriend), **James Finlayson** (Shipmate Fin), **Arthur Housman** (Drunkard), **Ruth Warren** (Mrs Addelquist), **James Morton** (Bartender at Denker's), **Tiny Sandford** ("Heavy" at the docks), **Del Henderson** (Judge Polk), **Ralf Harolde**, **Noel Madison** (Gangsters), **Harry Bernard** (Policeman), **Walter Taylor** (Snuffy).

Also appeared: Charlie Hall, Charles Bachman, Baldwin Cooke, Bob O'Conor, Bobby Dunn, Fred Holmes, Art Rowlands.

Misunderstandings abound for Stan and Ollie when their long-lost twin brothers, Alfie Laurel and Bert Hardy, hit town whilst on shore leave from the S S *Periwinkle*. Bert and Alf are entrusted to deliver a valuable pearl ring to their captain at Denker's Beer Garden, but when they arrive they become involved with two floozies. Unable to pay the bill, the sailors leave the ring as security while they go off to find their shipmate (James Finlayson), who is saving their pay so that they can become millionaires. While they are gone, Stan and Ollie enter the same beer garden with their wives and are immediately confronted by the gold-digging floozies who believe they have been stood up. The waiter demands payment of the girls' bill, and after Ollie reluctantly pays up, he is handed the ring which of course he knows nothing about. The wives, thinking that their husbands have been playing about, storm off so the boys decide to teach them a lesson by staying out all night. Bert and Alfie return to the beer garden, but when the waiter tells them that he's already handed the ring back, they think he has stolen it, and after refusing to leave the premises, are arrested. The wives hear about the arrests from a friend, and believing it to be their husbands, rush round to the courthouse to plead with the judge, who eventually agrees to release them. The foursome go for a night out at The Pirate Club, with Bert and Alfie thinking the girls are welfare workers. Stan and Ollie are also in the club and confusion reigns as the pair of twins are continually mistaken for each other. The ship's captain turns up as well and asks Stan and Ollie for the ring, but the conversation is overheard by two gangsters. Eager to get their hands on the valuable ring, the crooks invite the boys for a ride in their car, driving them to the docks and handing them over to a gang of heavies. Because they are

(Ollie) 'But you don't understand sir, that's Mr. Peter Cucumber, the big oil magnate.'
(Cop) 'I don't care if he's Mr. Dill Pickle, he's going to be searched.' (*ME AND MY PAL*)

unable to produce the goods, as Ollie had put the ring in Alfie's pocket thinking that he was Stan, they are given a cement footbath, eventually rolling off the wharf and into the dock. Just then Bert and Alfie appear, pursued by the captain and the police. Alfie finds the ring in his pocket and hands it to the captain, who is in the middle of winching Stan and Ollie out of the water. Thinking that he's seeing double, the captain runs off leaving the somewhat surprised sailors to winch their twin-brothers to dry land. With everything sorted out, the brothers head off to explain all to the wives, only for Ollie and Bert to fall into the dock.

The film was billed as "A Stan Laurel Production" although sources at the studios suspected that Stan's new title was merely a ploy to keep him happy during the ever increasing squabbles he was having with Hal Roach. The film marked the final appearance with the boys of Stanley "Tiny" Sandford, which ended a relationship started in their first Hal Roach film, 45 MINUTES FROM HOLLYWOOD.

ON THE WRONG TREK

Directed by **Charles Parrott & Harold Law**, Produced by **Hal Roach**, Filmed - Apr 1936, Released - Apr 18, 1936 by MGM, Running time - 2 reels.

With: **Charley Chase** (As himself), **Rosina Lawrence** (Mrs Chase), **Bonita Weber** (Mother-in-law), **Harry Bernard, Jack Hill, Bobby Burns, Dick Gilbert** (Hoboes at border), **Leo Willis, Bob Kortman** (Gang members), **Gertrude Sutton** (Office worker), **Harry Bowen** (Border cop), **Clarence Wilson** (New District Manager), **May Wallace** (His wife).

Also appeared: Charles McAvoy, Bob O'Conor, Lester Dorr.

Charley Chase, his wife and "know-it-all" mother-in-law are on their way to Los Angeles for a vacation. After passing a number of hitchhikers along the way (including Stan and Ollie), they run into what they think is a road accident. Charley stops despite his mother-in-law's comments that it looks like a scam for a hold-up. Sure enough "mother knows best" and Charley and his wife are relieved of their clothes as well as the car. The trio

What Was The Film When..?

Thelma Todd & Charley Chase
1905 - 1935   1893 - 1940

continue the journey in the robbers' battered old "Tin Lizzy" which soon runs out of petrol. They ask a couple picnicking at the side of the road for a spare can, but when Charley tries to syphon some fuel from the couple's car, it rolls down a bank, overturning at the bottom. Charley and family do the honourable thing and make a dash for it, only to reach California and be refused entry by a border cop, who mistakes them for hoboes. Heading back to Salt Lake City, and still 200 miles from home, the car explodes. When hitchhiking proves unsuccessful, they decide to use the same ploy as the robbers and pretend they've been in an accident. Unfortunately the police are wise to the racket, and when they run into Charley and his family strewn all over the road, they assume they are the gang responsible and arrest them. After spending the remainder of the vacation in jail, Charley returns to work, and is explaining to his work mates about his disastrous trip, when the new district manager arrives at the office. Again Charley is unlucky, as the manager turns out to be the owner of the overturned car who duly knocks him through the office door.

Charley Chase (real name Charles Parrott) starred and directed in one of the last shorts to be made at the Roach Studios, which was now geared to producing feature-length movies. Stan and Ollie would bid their farewells to Charley Chase by appearing very briefly during the film.

WAY OUT WEST

Directed by **James Horne**, Produced by **Stan Laurel for Hal Roach**, Edited by **Bert Jordan**, Filmed - Aug-Nov 1936, Released - Apr 16, 1937 by MGM, Running time - 65 minutes.

With: **James Finlayson** (Mickey Finn), **Sharon Lynne** (Lola Marcel), **Rosina Lawrence** (Mary Roberts), **Stanley Fields** (Sheriff), **Vivien Oakland** (Sheriff's wife, Molly), **James Morton** (Bartender), **Harry Bernard** (Man with sandwich).

Also appeared: Mary Gordon, May Wallace, Jack Hill, Sam Lufkin, Fred Toones, James Mason, The Avalon Boys (Chill Wills, Walter Trask, Don Brookins, Art Green), Dinah the mule.

The boys with Rosina Lawrence and Dinah the mule in WAY OUT WEST

Any Nuts?

Stan, Ollie and their trusty mule are on the way to Brushwood Gulch to deliver the deeds of a gold mine to Mary Roberts, the daughter of a friend who has passed away. They hitch a ride into town on the stagecoach, annoying the sheriff's wife so much during the journey, that they are ordered by her husband to leave town on the next stage. As the boys have never set eyes on Mary before, they are duped into handing the deeds over to saloon owner Mickey Finn and his wife, Lola Marcel, who is passed off as Mary. Only on leaving do they bump into the real heir, who is working in the saloon as a cleaner and general dogsbody. They snatch back the deeds and Stan hides the documents under his shirt, but is tickled so much by Lola trying to retrieve them, that he hands them over and they are locked in the safe. The intervention of the sheriff puts payed to any further attempts and the boys are run out of town. When night falls they return to the saloon, eventually breaking in through the cellar. They inform Mary of the goings-on and tell her to pack her bags, while they try to get back the deeds. Their noisy entrance alerts the saloon owner who finds the boys hiding in a piano. A struggle ensues and Finn is overpowered and forced at gunpoint to hand over the stolen documents. With the rightful owner now in possession, Mary and the boys head out of town and back home to Dixie.

WAY OUT WEST was regarded as one of Laurel and Hardy's finest features. It is remembered for their delightful soft-shoe-shuffle to The Avalon Boys' *At The Ball That's All,* **and Stan and Ollie's rendition of** *Trail Of The Lonesome Pine,* **which spent ten weeks in the British Pop Charts, entering in November 1975 and peaking at the No.2 slot (Queen's** *Bohemian Rhapsody* **prevented it from reaching the coveted No.1). Stan's deep voice-over in the song was provided by Avalon Boy, Chill Wills, with Rosina Lawrence performing the high pitched finale, after Ollie cracks Stan over the head with a mallet.**

PICK A STAR

Directed by **Edward Sedgwick**, Produced by **Hal Roach**, Edited by **William Terhune**, Filmed - Nov 1936 - Jan 1937, Released - May 21, 1937 by MGM, Running time - 70 minutes.

With: **Rosina Lawrence** (Miss Waterloo, Cecilia Moore), **Jack Haley** (Joe Jenkins), **Patsy Kelly** (Nellie Moore), **Mischa Auer** (Rinaldo Lopez), **James Finlayson** (Director at studios), **Russell Hicks** (Mr.

Stone), **Spencer Charters** (Judge Pike), **Walter Long** (Mexican cowboy), **Lyda Roberti** (Dagmar), **Sam Adams** (Sheriff), **Eddie Kane** (Albert, at the Colonial Club), **John Hyams** (Mr. McGregor), **Leila McIntyre** (Mrs McGregor), **Jack Norton** (The drunkard, Oscar), **Margie Roanberg** (Miss Gopher City), **Sam Lufkin** (Mexican hit by chair).

Also appeared: James Morton, Charlie Hall, Otto Fries, May Wallace, Wilma Cox, Bob O'Conor, Jack Hill, Mary Gordon, Felix Knight, James Burke, Charles Halton, Johnny Arthur, Joyce Compton.

Small time singer Cecilia Moore wins a talent contest and a part in a Hollywood movie. Her dreams of stardom however are shattered when the prize money is stolen, so Joe Jenkins, one of her biggest admirers, heads off to Hollywood to try and get her the big break. He lands himself a job at the exclusive Colonial Club, which is regularly frequented by famous movie stars and directors. Cecilia gets her own chance, when an aeroplane bound for Hollywood is forced to land in her home town, and a passenger reluctant to carry on with the journey, hands over two tickets. She persuades her sister Nellie to accompany her on the trip, where Cecilia soon becomes a romantic target for Rinaldo Lopez, a big movie star. In Hollywood the girls meet up with Joe, who pretends to keep company with all the famous celebrities at the club, while actually being no more than a kitchen hand. Later that evening, Rinaldo takes the girls to the club, where they realise the truth when Joe is sent to serve them at their table. He tries to save face by joining in the floor show, but is sacked when he messes up the act. Rinaldo takes the girls to the studios to meet some of the stars, including Stan and Ollie. Cecilia and Rinaldo leave, while Nellie stops behind to watch the boys take part in a bar room brawl with a tough Mexican cowboy (Walter Long) as they smash bottles over each other's heads. During a break in filming, Stan and Ollie explain to Nellie that the bottles used are just breakaway props and invite her to have a go. Unfortunately Nellie's bottle is real and she knocks out both the boys. Rinaldo has organised Cecilia a screen test and she is in make-up as Stan and Ollie relax off set, trying to outplay each other on a tiny harmonica. The contest ends when Ollie swallows the instrument, but that doesn't stop Stan from playing *Pop Goes The Weasel* by pressing different parts of Ollie's stomach! The screen test is not going well until Joe turns up to inspire his part it with flying colours.

(Stan) 'Yeh and then we floundered in a typhoid.' (*SONS OF THE DESERT*)

Any Nuts?

Stan and Ollie's two short sketches were filmed during production of WAY OUT WEST.

SWISS MISS

Directed by **John Blystone**, Produced by **Hal Roach**, Edited by **Bert Jordan**, Filmed - Dec 1937 - Jan 1938, Released - May 20, 1938 by MGM, Running time - 72 minutes.

With: **Walter Woolf King** (Victor Albert), **Della Lind** (Anna Hoepfel Albert), **Eric Blore** (Victor's aide, Edward), **Adia Kuznetzoff** (Chef Franzelhuber), **Ludovico Tomarchio** (Anton Luigi), **Charles Judels** (Emile the cheesemaker), **Charles Gemora** (The gorilla), **Eddie Kane, Anita Garvin** (Irate couple in doorway), **Jean de Briac** (Enrico), **George Sorel** (Chauffeur).

Also appeared: Sam Lufkin, Bob O'Conor, Winstead Weaver, Baldwin Cooke, Ed Brandenberg, Jack Hill, Dinah the mule.

The Alpen Hotel, high up in the Swiss mountains, is preparing for the visit of Victor Albert, a famous opera composer who is using the hotel as inspiration to write his greatest ever opera. As the opera is based on the Tyrol, he insists that the hotel staff dress up in native costume to achieve the proper ambience for his writing. Stan and Ollie arrive in the village as proprietors of The Miracle Mouse Trap Company, in the belief that, as Switzerland produces the most cheese, they must also have the most mice!! However, with no sales forthcoming the boys soon find themselves flat broke. Their luck seems to change when they sell their entire stock to a cheese maker for 5,000 Bovanian francs, and celebrate with a slap up meal at the hotel. After causing a big fuss over there being no apple pie on the menu they try to pay their bill, only to find their money worthless as there is no such place as Bovania. They are put to work in the hotel kitchens, with the manager threatening an extra day's work for every dish they break - and not surprisingly the days soon mount up. Meanwhile, Victor Albert's composing is not going well and he is frustrated further by the arrival of his wife, the famous opera singer Anna Hoepfel Albert. With his wife always receiving great acclaim for her singing, and Victor rarely any credit for his writing, he orders her

(Stan on the phone) 'Hello, this is me...yeh. Say listen, if you had a face like mine you'd punch me right in the nose, and I'm just the fellow that can do it.' (THE FIXER-UPPERS)

to leave, determined to be a success in his own right. Downstairs the boys bump into Anna, and when she hears their bad luck story she orders a double helping of everything on the menu and then refuses to pay. Her plan works a treat and she is put to work as a chambermaid. Stan and Ollie are in the yard plucking chickens when Stan takes an interest in the brandy hanging round the neck of a St. Bernard dog. His attempts at coaxing a drink from the dog fail until he fakes a snowstorm by throwing feathers in the air and pretends to be freezing to death. The dog gives up the liquor and in no time Stan has drained the barrel. Back in the hotel, and fed up with all the distractions, Victor asks for his piano to be moved to an isolated tree house further up the mountain trail. Stan and Ollie are commandeered for the job, with the already hair-raising trip up the trail made even more perilous due to Stan's inebriated state. They cross a rope bridge to the tree house, where they are confronted by a gorilla. The bridge breaks and sends both piano and gorilla plummeting into the gorge below, with Stan and Ollie just managing to scramble to safety. Next day is carnival day, and with the boys' help, Anna disguises herself as a gypsy, and is introduced to the crowd as "Romany Rose." Victor hears her singing and orders his aide to sign her up on contract, but he isn't fooled for long and soon realises that it's Anna, and the couple make up. With this, Stan and Ollie bid farewell to the hotel, and are just leaving when they are met by the gorilla swathed in bandages. The boys make a run for it but are stopped dead in their tracks when the gorilla hurls his crutch at them.

Charles Gemora, who had played the chimp in the film of the same name, returned to don the gorilla suit in SWISS MISS, a musical feature punctuated with Laurel and Hardy pantomime. Anita Garvin made a welcome return to play a prospective mouse trap customer, her first appearance in a Laurel and Hardy film since BE BIG in 1931. Baldwin Cooke left the Laurel and Hardy scene, with this his 30th and final appearance.

BLOCK-HEADS

Directed by **John Blystone**, Produced by **Hal Roach**, Edited by **Bert Jordan**, Filmed - Jun-Aug 1938, Released - Aug 19, 1938 by MGM, Running time - 58 minutes.

Any Nuts?

With: **Minna Gombell** (Mrs Hardy), **Patricia Ellis** (Mrs Gilbert), **Billy Gilbert** (Big-game hunter, Mr. Gilbert), **Jean del Val** (French pilot), **William Royle** (Officer in trenches), **James Finlayson** (Gent who wants to fight), **James Morton** (Man reading newspaper, James), **Harry Strang** (Desk clerk), **Patsy Moran** (Ollie's ex-girlfriend, Lulu), **Harry Earles** (Midget in lift), **Sam Lufkin** (Tough nut at soldiers home), **Tommy Bond** (Brat at top of stairs), **Harry Woods** (Brat's father), **Billy Bletcher** (Voice-over for midget in lift).

Also appeared: Ed Brandenberg, Jack Hill, Henry Hall, Max Hoffman Jnr.

The year is 1917 and the boys are in the trenches during World War One. Their unit is ordered over the top, leaving Stan behind to guard the post until relieved of duty. Some twenty years pass and with the war now just a memory, Stan is still faithfully guarding the post, surviving on a diet of beans. He is finally discovered when he nearly shoots down a French plane, whose pilot informs him of the war's end. Ollie meanwhile is happily married and celebrating his first wedding anniversary. On his way to buy his wife a present, he spots Stan's photo in the newspaper proclaiming him a hero. Ollie rushes over to the National Soldiers Home to find his long lost comrade reading in the gardens. Because of the awkward way in which Stan is sitting in a wheelchair, Ollie thinks that he's lost a leg. He invites Stan home for a slap up meal and carries him with great difficulty to his car, before discovering the truth about his non-existent disability. The car is blocked in by a lorry and with the driver nowhere to be seen Stan attempts to move the offending vehicle, succeeding only in dumping its load of sand over Ollie and the car. Things get worse when they arrive back at Ollie's apartment block as Stan tries to park the car in the automated garage, wrecking both car and garage in the process. Mrs Hardy is also none too pleased about cooking for another of her husband's dead beat pals, so she packs her bags and goes off to stay with her mother. Ollie decides to cook dinner himself, but blows up the kitchen whilst trying to light the gas stove. Mrs Gilbert from across the hall hears the explosion and offers to clean up the mess, only to get drenched for her troubles when Ollie spills a bowl of punch over her. With Mrs Gilbert locked out of her apartment, Ollie loans her a pair of his pyjamas just as Mrs Hardy returns having found the wrecked car, and now the apartment in the same

(Ollie) 'Tell me that again.' (Stan) 'Well...if you caught a fish...and whoever you sold it to they wouldn't have to pay for it. And the profits...could...they'd go to the fish...' *(TOWED IN A HOLE)*

state. Mrs Gilbert is quickly bundled into a trunk as the Hardys begin a fierce argument. Mr. Gilbert, a big-game hunter, arrives on the scene with the quarrel in full flow. Stan spills the beans about the lady in the trunk, prompting Gillbert to boast about some of his own conquests around the world, including a tribe of blondes in Borneo. On hearing this, his wife rises from the trunk to face her philandering husband. Mr. Gilbert chases the boys outside brandishing his new elephant gun and when he lets off a shot outside the apartment block, it sends scores of half-dressed men leaping from every window.

BLOCK-HEADS was the last Laurel and Hardy/Hal Roach/MGM film and contained a re-worked version of the 1929 film UNACCUSTOMED AS WE ARE, faithfully following the original plot. The final moments of the film were also borrowed from the silent film WE FAW DOWN. Following a contract dispute between Stan and Hal Roach, Ollie played the part of a country doctor, Henry Tibbitt, in the 1939 film ZENOBIA* which also featured Harry Langdon and fuelled rumours that Laurel and Hardy were no more. It was Ollie's first film without Stan since 1928. The new Hardy/Langdon partnership lasted for just one film, as Stan settled his differences with Roach and the boys signed new short term contracts.

*The Roach film ZENOBIA was produced by A. Edward Sutherland, directed by Gordon Douglas and edited by Bert Jordan.

A CHUMP AT OXFORD (European Version)

Directed by **Alfred Goulding**, Produced by **Hal Roach**, Edited by **Bert Jordan**, Filmed - Jun-Sep 1939, Released - Feb 16, 1940 by United Artists, Running time - 63 minutes (US version 42 minutes, longer version released 1941).

With: **Wilfred Lucas** (Dean Williams), **James Finlayson** ("Baldy" Vandevere), **Anita Garvin** (Mrs Vandevere), **Gerald Rogers** (Johnson), **Charlie Hall** (Hector), **Peter Cushing** (Jones), **Frank Baker** (Jenkins), **Victor Kendall** (Cecil), **Gerald Fielding** (Brown), **Jack Heasley** (Hodges), **Forbes Murray** (Bank president, James Finlayson),

Any Nuts?

Forrester Harvey (Meredith the valet), **Harry Bernard** (Policeman at dinner party), **Jean de Briac** (Pierre the chef), **Vivien Oakland** (Receptionist at Sterling's), **Eddie Borden** ("Ghost" in maze), **Rex Lease** (Bank robber), **Sam Lufkin** (Driver of street cleaner).

Also appeared: Stanley Blystone, Alec Harford, James Millican.

Down to their last six dollars, Stan and Ollie are so desperate for work, they accept a job as maid and butler, with Stan persuaded to take on the role of "Agnes" the maid. He soon turns the Vandevere's posh dinner party into a complete shambles when he spills the hors d'oeuvres into Mrs Vandevere's lap, and then gets drunk after consuming too many cocktails. The final straw comes when he is asked to serve the salad without dressing, and duly obliges by serving it in his underwear! Not surprisingly, the host is not impressed and runs the boys out of the house brandishing his shotgun. Re-employed as street cleaners, Stan and Ollie inadvertently foil a bank raid while on their lunch break, when the robber slips on Stan's discarded banana skin. They are rewarded for their heroics with the best education money can buy - two places at Oxford University. Shortly after arriving on campus, the pair are set upon by student pranksters, who give them the "royal initiation" by sending them into the maze, where they spend a scary night with a student dressed as a ghost. In the morning they are shown to their quarters, which really belong to the dean. They are settling down in their new surroundings, when the dean himself discovers them and orders them to leave. Thinking this is another student rib, they end up in a pillow fight with him. Only when it becomes obvious that he's genuine do Stan and Ollie explain the situation and the culprits are expelled. In their proper quarters, Meredith the valet instantly recognises Stan as being the returning Lord Paddington, Oxford's greatest ever scholar and athlete, who had wandered away from the university some years earlier, suffering from amnesia after being struck on the head by the window frame whilst receiving the plaudits for defeating Cambridge. The boys laugh off Meredith's ridiculous claim thinking it is yet another prank, and that Meredith is just a touch nutty. Because of the expulsions, Stan and Ollie are found guilty of snitching, a violation of the ethics of the student body, and the students storm their quarters determined to hound them out. The boys are just about to make their escape through the window, when Stan is struck on the head by the frame. Meredith's claims prove true, as this causes Stan to revert to being Lord Paddington, who swiftly disposes of the students by throwing them out of the

(Ollie) 'Er excuse me please, my ear is full of milk.' *(GOING BYE-BYE!)*

window. Even Ollie and the dean don't escape his wrath as they suffer the same fate. Ollie is taken on as Stan's personal servant, enduring much humiliation including the nickname "Fattie." It isn't long before Lord Paddington has reclaimed his title as Oxford's greatest student, even offering Einstein advice regarding his theory! Ollie's patience finally snaps and he declares that he's returning to America. Seemingly unconcerned, Stan is milking the acclaim of the students at his window when he is again struck on the head by the frame, this time returning him to his normal self and back into Ollie's friendship.

Anita Garvin's final film with Stan and Ollie, repeating her role from the 1928 film FROM SOUP TO NUTS for the European version. The idea for this feature came from A YANK AT OXFORD made in 1937 starring Robert Taylor as a brash American upsetting the traditionalists at Oxford University. Appearing in A CHUMP AT OXFORD was a young Peter Cushing who played one of the student pranksters. After appearing, Cushing's own film career took off, and before long he had established himself as the undisputed King of Horror.

THE FLYING DEUCES

Directed by **A. Edward Sutherland**, Produced by **Boris Morros**, Edited by **Jack Dennis**, Filmed - Jul/Aug 1939, Released - Oct 20, 1939 by RKO, Running time - 69 minutes.

With: **Jean Parker** (Georgette), **Reginald Gardiner** (Francois), **Charles Middleton** (Commandant), **James Finlayson** (Jailer), **Michael Visaroff** (Innkeeper), **Jean del Val** (Sergeant), **Rychard Cramer** (Vegetable truck driver), **Arthur Housman** (Drunk legionnaire).

Also appeared: Frank Clarke, Eddie Borden, Sam Lufkin, Monica Bannister, Bonnie Bannon, Christine Cabanne, Mary-Jane Carey.

While holidaying in Paris, Ollie falls head-over-heels in love with Georgette, the innkeeper's daughter, unaware that she is already happily married to Francois, a captain in the Foreign Legion. With his proposal of marriage politely turned down and with nothing seemingly to live for, Ollie decides to take Stan's off-the-cuff advice and drown himself. By the riverside Stan is persuaded to jump in too, but both are prevented from doing so by

Any Nuts?

Francois, who advises them to join the Legion in order for Ollie to forget his heartache. Thinking it will take only a few days, the boys join up. Once in uniform they soon realise that this is not the life for them, especially when they have to wash and iron a mountainous pile of clothes for a measly three cents a day. Enough is enough when they are asked to prepare a truck load of vegetables for supper. In an instant Ollie forgets all about Georgette and they decide to leave. With bags packed they head off for the railway depot, but on the way, Ollie bumps into Georgette who has flown into camp to join her husband. Thinking she has changed her mind over his proposal, Ollie is in the middle of a warm embrace, when Francois arrives to pick her up, resulting in Ollie being promised untold miseries if he is ever caught with his wife again. The camp commandant catches up with them and they are arrested for desertion and sentenced to be shot at sunrise. During the night a note is tossed through the cell window, informing them of a trapdoor in the cell, leading to a tunnel and freedom. With the jailer asleep, the boys make their escape crawling along the dark tunnel. When it caves in they have to dig upwards and find themselves in a cellar underneath Georgette's living quarters. Georgette faints when Stan sneezes as he and Ollie hide in her wardrobe. Ollie tries to revive her as Francois walks in on them, so the boys are forced to make a quick getaway by crashing headfirst through the bedroom window. As an extensive search of the barracks takes place, the boys hide in an aeroplane. Just when they think the coast is clear, Stan accidentally starts the engine. The plane careers out of control around the airfield, scattering legionnaires in all directions, before finally becoming airborne. Several near misses later, they crash and Stan emerges from the wreckage as the only survivor, as Ollie floats up to heaven. It isn't long however before Stan meets up with his pal again, standing in a field, re-incarnated as a horse complete with derby and toothbrush moustache!

With the American version of A CHUMP AT OXFORD complete, the boys were loaned to independent producer Boris Morros, to make their second Foreign Legion picture, which contained Stan's delightful and amusing rendition of *The World Is Waiting For The Sunrise* played on the springs of his cell bed. On returning to the Roach Studios, the boys shot an extra two reels for A CHUMP AT OXFORD to satisfy the European demand for their films (where they were regarded as top-of-the-bill attractions, unlike in the States, where some critics and film reviewers of the day found it hard work to write anything complimentary about any Laurel and Hardy release).

(Stan) 'What'll we have for dinner?' (Ollie) 'How about a plate of beans and a pot of steaming hot coffee?' (Stan) 'Swell – you sure know how to plan a meal.' (THEM THAR HILLS)

What Was The Film When..?

SAPS AT SEA

Directed by **Gordon Douglas**, Produced by **Hal Roach**, Edited by **William Ziegler**, Filmed - Nov/Dec 1939, Released - May 3, 1940 by United Artists, Running time - 57 minutes.

With: **Rychard Cramer** (Nick Grainger), **James Finlayson** (Doctor J. H. Finlayson), **Ben Turpin** (Cross-eyed plumber), **Harry Hayden** (Factory boss), **Charlie Hall** (Desk clerk), **Eddie Conrad** (Professor O'Brien), **Patsy Moran** (Lady on switchboard), **Robert McKenzie** (Captain McKenzie), **Mary Gordon** (Neighbour across the hall), **Harry Bernard** (Harbour Patrol captain), **Eddie Borden** (Nervous breakdown victim).

Also appeared: Gene Morgan, Charles Bachman, Jack Hill, Patsy O'Byrne, Sam Lufkin, Narcissus the goat.

Working in the test department of the Sharp and Pierce Horn Company, Ollie suffers a nervous breakdown due to the constant noise, with the G-minor horn blamed as the main culprit. He is sent home where the doctor diagnoses "Hornophobia." The doctor prescribes plenty of peace and goat's milk to drink, with an ocean voyage suggested as a cure. As Ollie is a bad sailor, a compromise is reached and he and Stan rent a boat moored at the dock. At the quayside, along with their pet goat Narcissus, the boys clamber aboard their boat, *Prickly Heat*, safe in the knowledge that the boat is securely fastened. Stan is scolded for bringing along his trombone, as Ollie states that the sound of a horn makes him fighting mad with an urge to kill. They settle down for the night not knowing an escaped killer, Nick Grainger, is hiding on board, having been tracked by the police and cornered at the docks. The boys awake next morning to find themselves adrift at sea after the goat had chewed through the mooring rope during the night. The killer introduces himself and gives the boys new nicknames of "Dizzy" (Ollie) and "Dopey" (Stan). Grainger orders them to prepare him a meal, so they use the opportunity to try and poison him and claim the $5,000 reward for his capture, by making the meal of inedible lookalikes such as string for spaghetti, grated soap as cheese and pieces of sponge for meatballs. Unfortunately Grainger is wise to the trick and makes the boys eat it instead. Stan then has a brainwave and starts to blow his trombone, making Ollie so mad he knocks the killer cold. The Harbour Patrol

(Stan) 'What are you going to do, cook something?' (Mrs Hardy to Ollie)
'Yes, I'm going to cook his goose.' (THICKER THAN WATER)

Any Nuts ?

Harry Langdon and Ollie seem bemused by the script from the film ZENOBIA, the partnership fuelled rumours that Stan and Ollie were no more

(Top) Nick Grainger (Rychard Cramer) gets tough with Ollie in SAPS AT SEA, and below Harry Bernard becomes another victim of "hornophobia"

(Top) The Hardy's wedding anniversary is about to be spoiled in BLOCK-HEADS, and below Stan attempting to "wiggle his ears" for Meredith the valet (Forrester Harvey) in A CHUMP AT OXFORD

arrives, and when the captain asks how they apprehended Grainger, Stan makes the mistake of showing him by again blowing his trombone. This time the captain becomes the victim of Ollie's rage, resulting in the boys being arrested and thrown into the same cell as Nick Grainger.

Director Gordon Douglas had also tasted life on the other side of the camera and had appeared in several Roach films, including bit parts in CHICKENS COME HOME, COME CLEAN, ONE GOOD TURN, PARDON US, BEAU HUNKS and ON THE LOOSE. Stan and Ollie's last Laurel and Hardy/Hal Roach production, SAPS AT SEA, saw the boys bidding their farewells to old buddies Charlie Hall, James Finlayson, Jack Hill and Harry Bernard who were making their final bow in Laurel and Hardy films. The boys' contracts expired in April 1940 and Laurel and Hardy Feature Productions, which Stan and Ollie had formed in October 1939, waited for a film offer, but none were forthcoming as they were initially shunned by all the major film companies. Until this time Laurel and Hardy had remained virtually unrivalled as a comedy duo, but at the beginning of the 1940's a rival for their crown emerged. Abbott and Costello's often vulgar, "machine-gun-fire" slapstick proved a smash hit at the box office, and their army comedy BUCK PRIVATES certainly backed up their claims. Twelve months passed with several ventures in the pipeline, before in April 1941 Stan and Ollie signed a one picture agreement with 20th Century-Fox with the potentially lucrative option of making ten films over a five year span. This, plus the fact that they were free to work for other interested parties without obligation to 20th Century-Fox, all added up to what seemed a good deal. Delighted with the arrangement and the unlimited resources available at a major studio (unlike Roach's limited budget), the boys viewed the deal as an excellent career move. Stan however didn't realise that the almost total control he had enjoyed at the Roach Studios, would not apply here and the boys would not be allowed any creative contributions to their films, other than performing in front of the cameras. The boys had become part of a studio factory which regularly churned out a picture every week. The Fox studio system was not about to change just because the boys disagreed with the way their films were being handled. This attitude was to become evident in their first Fox release, GREAT GUNS. Future films would spiral into a nose dive of mediocrity, a situation from which Stan and Ollie's film careers would never recover.

Their Final Reel

Great Guns to Atoll K

Their Final Reel

GREAT GUNS

5+

Directed by **Monty Banks**, Produced by **Sol M. Wurtzel**, Edited by **Al de Gaetano**, Filmed - Jul/Aug 1941, Released - Oct 10, 1941 by 20th Century Fox, Running time - 74 minutes.

With: **Dick Nelson** (Dan Forrester), **Sheila Ryan** (Virginia "Ginger" Hammond), **Edmund MacDonald** (Sergeant Hippo), **Ludwig Stossel** (Dr. Hugo Schickel), **Mae Marsh** (Aunt Martha), **Ethel Griffies** (Aunt Agatha), **Kane Richmond** (Captain Baker), **Russell Hicks** (General Burns), **Alan Ladd** (Soldier at photo shop), **Irving Bacon** (Postman), **Charles Arndt** (Medical doctor), **Charles Trowbridge** (Colonel Ridley), **Dick Rich** (Post Cook), **Pierre Watkin** (Colonel Wayburn).

Also appeared: Chet Brandenberg, Penelope the crow.

Stan and Ollie are man-servants to millionaire Dan Forrester, who is, according to the family doctor, suffering from every ailment and allergy known to man. When Dan receives his draft papers for the army, the doctor and Dan's doting aunts do their utmost to persuade him not to attend the medical, yet to everyone's surprise he is passed fit, much to his delight. The boys, accompanied by Stan's pet crow Penelope, join up too so they can look after their master. They arrive at Fort Merritt with Stan and Ollie overly protective towards Dan's every move. He then becomes romantically involved with a girl on camp called "Ginger" who works at Hammond's Photo Shop, but in doing so upsets the tough Sergeant Hippo who has also fallen for her charms. After a lucky escape on the rifle range, the boys learn about Dan's affair, and thinking that the romance might kill him, and that "Ginger" is nothing more than a gold digger, set about finishing it. They dress up as rich tycoons and try to pay off the girl, after telling her that Dan is bankrupt, but she throws them out as she isn't the least bit interested in his wealth. Sergeant Hippo, with a little assistance from Stan and Ollie, throws Dan in the guard house. The boys then take part in war game manoeuvres where they find themselves on patrol for the white army. They drive through a mine field and are bombed with flour before they are eventually captured by the enemy, the blue's, who put them to work building a bridge. Dan hears about the boys' capture and bets the sergeant $50 that the white army still win the day. He escapes on a garbage truck and with Penelope's help, leads the white's straight to the blue camp to win the war for their side.

(Stan) 'You can't go - you're sick - you're all in a heap.' *(BE BIG)*

What Was The Film When..?

Gags as old as the hills and the shameful plundering of previous Laurel and Hardy sketches, summed up their first Fox release, which would tend to be the norm for all of their six Fox films (Stan would later comment how ashamed he was of the Fox pictures and his dislike for the people concerned). Ad-libbing, such an important feature of Laurel and Hardy/Roach films, was now a thing of the past, as the boys were made to stick rigidly to the script in hand. Despite this, GREAT GUNS did well enough at the box office to warrant another Fox film.

A-HAUNTING WE WILL GO

Directed by **Alfred Werker**, Produced by **Sol M. Wurtzel**, Edited by **Alfred Day**, Filmed - Mar/Apr 1942, Released - Aug 7, 1942 by 20th Century Fox, Running time - 67 minutes.

With: **Harry Jansen** (Dante the Magician), **Sheila Ryan** (Margo), **John Shelton** (Tommy White), **George Lynn** (Darby Mason), **Elisha Cook Jnr.** (Frank Lucas), **Don Costello** (Doc Lake), **Addison Richards** (Attorney/FBI agent), **Edward Gargan** (Lieutenant Foster), **Lou Lubin** (Dixie).

Also appeared: James Bush, Robert Emmett Keane, Richard Lane, Mantan Moreland, Willie Best.

After spending a night in the Hamilton police cells, the boys are given just six hours to leave town, or face sixty days hard labour. They manage to get themselves a job transporting a corpse to Dayton, unaware that the coffin contains the very-much-alive gangster Darby Mason, who stands to inherit $250,000 if he can reach his destination whilst evading the police. Stan and Ollie catch the afternoon train, not knowing the coffin they are to escort has been mixed up with a prop belonging to Dante the Magician, travelling on the same train. During the journey the boys are fleeced of all their money when they are conned into buying a so-called money making gadget called an "Inflato" having seen a couple of tricksters apparently change a $1 note into a $100. The boys order a meal but when they are unable to pay the bill, and about to be thrown off at the next station, Dante comes to their rescue and settles the bill. In Dayton the gangsters have set up their headquarters in a sanitarium, but when the coffin arrives all it contains is an imitation mummy and some flysheets for Dante's show. They head off for The Temple Theatre where the magician is performing, with Stan and Ollie now in his employment, after helping him out whilst rehearsing an illusion. The boys are cornered by Darby's gang demanding to know the whereabouts of the real coffin. Threatened at gunpoint they escape onto the stage with the show in full swing, and are incorporated into the act, bringing the house down with their attempt at the Indian rope trick. The coffin, suspended from the theatre ceiling as part of the act, is noticed by the gangsters. Realising the game is up, they try to make their getaway, but fall through a trapdoor and into a lions cage. Dante, with Stan's help, then performs the Egyptian transfer trick involving the coffin. However, when it is lowered to the stage and opened, they find the body of Doc Lake, a member of the gang who had been shot dead by Darby Mason for double-crossing him. Darby also falls in with the lions, as Dante and his stage manager are accused of the murder. The real assassin and his gang are soon discovered and saved just in time from being devoured. The police arrive to make the arrests, while Darby is taken away by an FBI agent who had been posing as an attorney, inventing the inheritance scam in order to flush him out. Stan meanwhile has disappeared, but is found by Ollie, rolling around backstage, miniaturised inside an egg.

Stan and Ollie's characters, perfected during thirteen years under Hal Roach, were virtually unrecognisable in the first two Fox films. Situations from previous Laurel and Hardy films were again used, including a sketch taken from the silent short WRONG AGAIN, where a broken statue is re-assembled with the pieces facing the wrong way. Stan and Ollie then signed a one picture agreement with MGM who had previously distributed their Hal Roach films.

AIR RAID WARDENS

Directed by **Edward Sedgwick**, Produced by **B. F. Zeidman**, Edited by **Irvine Warburton**, Filmed - Dec 1942/Jan 1943, Released - Apr 1943 by MGM, Running time - 67 minutes.

With: **Horace McNally** (Dan Madison), **Howard Freeman** (J. P. Norton), **Jacqueline White** (Peggy Parker), **Edgar Kennedy** (Removal man, Joe Bledsoe), **Paul Stanton** (Captain Biddle), **Donald Meek** (Eustace Middling), **Nella Walker** (Millicent Norton), **Russell Hicks** (Major

What Was The Film When..?

Scanlon), **Don Costello** (Heydrich), **Phil Van Zandt** (Herman), **Frederic Worlock** (Otto).

Also appeared: Henry O'Neil, Robert Emmett O'Connor, William Tannen, Charles Coleman, Milton Kibbee, Forrest Taylor, Edward Hearn, Bobby Burns, Daisy the dog.

Stan and Ollie shut down their bicycle shop in the small town of Huxton to go and help "Uncle Sam" win the war. After being rejected by all the services, they return to their shop where they form a partnership with Eustace Middling, new in town selling radios. The boys' urge to do something for the war effort sees them join the town's Civil Defence, but during a practical demonstration, the bank president, acting as a volunteer, almost becomes a real life victim when Stan's carelessness renders him unconscious and submerged under a lorry load of sand. The pair are given one last chance and while out on patrol they tangle with a tough cookie (Edgar Kennedy) who refuses to abide by the blackout regulations. As usual things get out of hand and the boys are knocked cold. When found, they are accused of being drunk, and asked to hand in their equipment. Inconsolable, they return to their shop where Stan stumbles upon two German spies snooping about inside. The boys hide in the boot of the spies' car and are driven to their headquarters, just out of town. They break in through a top floor window, to find their partner Eustace Middling in cohorts with the spies. They soon learn of the Germans' plan to blow up the town's magnesium plant at five o'clock that day, the same time the Civil Defence and the majority of the townsfolk are involved in a mock incident, set up for the visiting Major Scanlon. Stan and Ollie are discovered, but manage to slip their guard and escape in a car loaned from a scrap yard. The Germans arrive at the magnesium plant pretending to be looking for work, and knock out the guards before planting the explosives. Ollie rings up the Civil Defence warning them of the spies' intentions. Thinking it is a surprise incident arranged by the major, the Civil Defence rush round to catch the spies, just as they are about to carry out the deadly deed, and for once Stan and Ollie are deemed heroes.

Not even the appearance of Stan and Ollie's old foe Edgar Kennedy could save AIR RAID WARDENS from being another desperately disappointing film, with re-worked gags from BLOCK-HEADS and HELPMATES, as well as the main plot of the picture following the lines of the 1938 George Formby film IT'S IN THE AIR. MGM this

time failed to produce a half-decent script or capable director (Edward Sedgwick had even worked with the boys in the film PICK A STAR). They returned to 20th Century-Fox for their next film, after being promised a more suitable director and better script writers.

JITTERBUGS

Directed by **Malcolm St. Clair**, Produced by **Sol M. Wurtzel**, Edited by **Norman Colbert**, Filmed - Feb/Mar 1943, Released - Jun 11, 1943 by 20th Century Fox, Running time - 74 minutes.

With: **Robert Bailey** (Chester Wright), **Vivian Blaine** (Susan Cowan), **Douglas Fowley** (Bennett), **Robert Emmett Keane** (Corcoran), **Noel Madison** (Tony Queen), **Lee Patrick** (Dorcas), **Francis Ford** (Stooge in the crowd), **Anthony Caruso** (Queen's henchman, Mike), **Charles Halton** (Samuel J. Cass, editor of Midvale Daily Planet).

Travelling musicians Stan and Ollie run out of petrol in the middle of nowhere and are rescued by con-man entrepreneur, Chester Wright, who convinces them he can perform miracles by changing a gallon of water into gasoline with the aid of his "wonder pill." They form a partnership, with the boys given the job of selling the phoney pill at the Midvale Carnival. Their music soon draws a large crowd and with the help of a stooge in the audience they do a roaring trade, that is until the pill is exposed as a fake. They are about to be lynched when Chester, posing as a detective, arrives on the scene and "arrests" them, before escorting them out of town. Chester and the boys then become involved with local girl Susan Cowan, whose mother has been swindled out of a large sum of money in a real estate deal, when the envelope containing the money was switched with another containing cut-up newspaper. They decide to help recover the money, and with Ollie disguised as Colonel Bixby, a Texan "Casanova" and Stan as his faithful valet "Potts," they recover half the cash from Corcoran, one of the crooks. Another plan is hatched to get the rest back from Malcolm Bennett who runs a moored showboat. Susan gets a job on the boat as a singer, while Stan dresses up as Susan's rich Aunt Emily from Boston, pretending to be interested in buying into the show. A deal is struck and they swindle the crooks by switching the envelopes, with Chester entrusted with the one containing the cash. Unfortunately the crooks see through Stan and Ollie's elaborate disguises and unable

Vivian Blaine in JITTERBUGS

to return the cash as Chester has disappeared, they are taken aboard the boat. Thinking they have all been hoodwinked, the crooks imprison the boys in the boiler house, but they manage to escape and save Susan from the evil clutches of gang leader Tony Queen. The boat then breaks its moorings and with Stan and Ollie at the helm, is soon out of control. However, Chester's arrival on the police launch saves the day, and his explanation to Susan that the money is safely back with her mother clears his name. The happy couple leave as the boys dive overboard to escape the pursuing hoodlums.

Malcolm St. Clair was in the chair for JITTERBUGS having previously gained comedy experience working for Mack Sennett and receiving notable acclaim for his work on some of Buster Keaton's finest films. He would direct four Laurel and Hardy/Fox features, with JITTERBUGS arguably the best of their post-Roach films. Noel Madison would repeat his gangster role from OUR RELATIONS.

THE TREE IN A TEST TUBE

Directed by **Charles McDonald**, Produced by the US Dept. of Agriculture Forest Service at 20th Century-Fox, Edited by **Boris Vermont**, Filmed - Feb/Mar 1943, Released - Early 1943, Running time - 1 reel.

Narrated by **Pete Smith & Lee Vickers**.

Pete Smith is narrating a documentary about the importance of wood in the war effort, and enlists the help of Stan and Ollie as they walk down the street. He asks them if they are carrying any wood, so Stan obliges by turning out his pockets to reveal many wood-related products, including a pipe and an imitation leather wallet that contains a pair of rayon stockings. Ollie even knocks on Stan's head to see if that's wooden! With his pockets emptied, Stan opens his small suitcase that also contains several wood-related items such as note paper, envelopes and a book of matches. Much to Ollie's amusement, Stan tries to hide a rather loud pair of rayon shorts. Pete Smith thanks the boys for their help, but as they pack up the suitcase, their car trundles down the slope and they have to give chase. The documentary ends with Lee Vickers carrying on the story about the importance of wood in helping to win the war.

(Stan) 'Well blow me down with an anchovy.' (*THE BOHEMIAN GIRL*)

Stan and Ollie's silent part in THE TREE IN A TEST TUBE was filmed during a lunch break while shooting JITTERBUGS, and was, along with THE ROGUE SONG, the only Laurel and Hardy film to be shot in colour.

THE DANCING MASTERS

Directed by **Malcolm St. Clair**, Produced by **Lee Marcus**, Edited by **Norman Colbert**, Filmed - Jun 1943, Released - Nov 19, 1943 by 20th Century Fox, Running time - 63 minutes.

With: **Trudy Marshall** (Trudy Harlan), **Robert Bailey** (Grant Lawrence), **Matt Briggs** (Wentworth Harlan), **Robert Mitchum** (Insurance trickster), **Margaret Dumont** (Mrs Harlan), **Allan Lane** (George Worthing), **Charley Rogers** (Butler), **Emory Parnell** (Featherstone), **Robert Emmett Keane** (Auctioneer), **Hank Mann** (Grocer), **Daphne Pollard** (Watching daughter at Dancing School).

The boys are proprietors of The Arthur Hurry School of Dancing that faces closure due to a lack of funds. To make matters worse, they are visited by extortionists who bully them into taking out an accident insurance policy. The salesmen leave with their easy pickings just as the police arrive to arrest them. A pupil at the school, Trudy Harlan, visits her father's weapons factory to see her beau, Grant Lawrence, who has invented a revolutionary ray gun. Mr. Harlan is not keen on Grant, and is lining up his daughter to wed George Worthing, soon to be his vice-president at the factory. Grant gets into a disagreement with Worthing on the factory floor and is fired. At home, Stan and Ollie are visited by the rent collector, Featherstone, who gives them until noon to pay up or face the closure of the school. Left with no alternative the boys draw out their life savings. On their way to pay off the debt they call in at an auction, and end up bidding for a grandfather clock on behalf of a lady who has left her money at home. When the lady fails to return, they have to use up all their savings to buy the clock, only to see it crushed by a truck when they put it down for a moment in the street. Later, Trudy calls round asking them to demonstrate Grant's new invention to her father and his board of directors. Posing as Professor Gorp, Stan demonstrates the gun which proves a big success, that is until the ray gun is left switched on and sets the Harland house ablaze, before exploding. Feeling responsible, the boys try to redeem

(Stan) 'Say listen – I've just got a couple of tickets for tonight for the Cement Workers Bazaar, can you come along? We might win a prize – they're going to give away a steam shovel.' *(THEIR FIRST MISTAKE)*

themselves by raising the $10,000 needed to re-finance Grant's invention. Ollie remembers the insurance policy, and then goes to great lengths to arrange an accident for Stan, only to pay a visit to the County Hospital himself, after breaking a leg while riding a roller-coaster on a runaway bus! Ollie's efforts however have all been in vain, as Mr. Harlan fires George Worthing for trying to steal Grant's ideas, and much to Trudy's delight, offers to finance the ray gun himself.

Yet another film filled with material lifted from previous Laurel and Hardy films, including THE BATTLE OF THE CENTURY, HOG WILD, COUNTY HOSPITAL and THICKER THAN WATER. In fact the auctioneer's sketch from THICKER THAN WATER (1935) was so similar, it could easily have been spliced into THE DANCING MASTERS without any discernible difference. A large proportion of the film is taken up by a meaningless party thrown by Trudy while her parents are out of town. Robert Mitchum, just beginning his movie career, plays a small part as an insurance trickster.

THE BIG NOISE

Directed by **Malcolm St. Clair**, Produced by **Sol M. Wurtzel**, Edited by **Norman Colbert**, Filmed - Apr 1944, Released - Sep 1944 by 20th Century Fox, Running time - 74 minutes.

With: **Arthur Space** (Professor Alva Hartley), **Robert Blake** (Egbert Hartley), **Esther Howard** (Aunt Sophie), **Robert Dudley** (Mr. Hartley Snr.), **Veda Ann Borg** (Mrs Charlton), **Doris Merrick** (Mrs Charlton's niece, Evelyn), **Phil Van Zandt** (Dutchie), **Frank Fenton** (Charlton), **James Bush** (Jim Hartman), **George Melford** (The butler, Mugridge), **Edgar Dearing** (Motorbike cop), **Harry Hayden** (Digby at Patent Office), **Jack Norton** (Drunkard on train).

Also appeared: Francis Ford, Charles Wilson, Del Henderson, Selmer Jackson, Julie Carter, Billy Bletcher.

Eccentric Professor Alva Hartley has invented a revolutionary bomb nicknamed "The Big Noise," which he hopes will help bring a premature end to the war. A gang of crooks moves in next door planning to steal jewellery belonging to Hartley's rich Aunt Sophie. The professor thinks the gang are after his bomb so rings a detective agency to get some protection for his invention. Stan and Ollie working as janitors at the agency answer the call, and as the detectives on the books are on government business, take on the job themselves. Arriving at the Hartley household for their live-in position, they soon become the victims of Hartley's mischievous son, Egbert, and the gadget-filled house, with Ollie also a romantic target for man-mad Aunt Sophie. The professor receives a phone call from the Patent Office requesting him to bring the bomb to Washington as the War Department are interested in the device. The gang however are now wise to the invention and two of the crooks, believing it to be more lucrative than the jewellery, plan to steal it and sell it to the enemy. Stan and Ollie are sent to Washington by train carrying a dummy bomb concealed in Stan's concertina, hoping to throw the robbers off the trail, while Hartley delivers the real bomb himself. Unfortunately the bombs have become mixed up, with the boys in possession of the real thing. After changing trains, the boys find out that the Washington-bound train is delayed, so to try and save time, they go to the airfield hoping to catch a plane instead. They hide from their pursuers in an old plane, not knowing that it is radio controlled, and is being used by the army gunnery units for target practice. The plane takes off and is shot to pieces, forcing the boys to parachute over the sea. As they descend, they spot an enemy submarine below, which Stan destroys when he drops the bomb on it!

More re-worked material in abundance, this time from BERTH MARKS (the cramped train berth scene), OLIVER THE EIGHTH, HABEAS CORPUS and WRONG AGAIN. The script writers were so lacking in new ideas, they even used a gag from the previous film THE DANCING MASTERS (involving the front door and the telephone). Edgar Dearing, Billy Bletcher and Del Henderson, who had appeared with the boys during their Hal Roach days, returned to play small parts in the film.

NOTHING BUT TROUBLE

Directed by **Sam Taylor**, Produced by **B.F. Zeidman**, Edited by **Conrad Nervig**, Filmed - Oct 1944, Released - Mar 1945 by MGM, Running time - 70 minutes.

With: **David Leland** (King Christopher), **Mary Boland** (Mrs Elvira Hawkley), **Philip Merivale** (Prince Saul), **Henry O'Neil** (Mr. Basil

Hawkley), **John Warburton** (Ronetz), **Matthew Boulton** (Prince Prentiloff), **Connie Gilchrist** (Mrs Flannagan), **Jean de Briac** (French restaurant proprietor), **Robert Emmett Homans** (Jailer), **William Frambe** (Passenger on liner).

Also appeared: Paul Porcasi, Joe Yule, Eddie Dunn, Forbes Murray, Ray Teal, Gary Owen, Robert Emmett O'Connor, Chester Clute.

"1932 - When jobs were as hard to find as a girdle on a welder."

Unemployed Stan and Ollie, descendants from a long line of butlers and chefs, decide to try for a job abroad. Returning some twelve years later and with jobs now ten-a-penny, the boys are snapped up by the wealthy Mrs Elvira Hawkley, to serve at her royal dinner party, which is to be attended by the young exiled King Christopher of Orlandia and his evil uncle, Prince Saul, who plans to have him abducted and then blame it on their political opponents. Saul's secretary, Ronetz, takes the King to the park where the dastardly deed is to take place, but the King evades his abductors when he becomes involved in a game of football. Stan and Ollie are walking through the park after purchasing groceries for the party and are asked to referee the game. The King and the boys become friends when he helps them steal a piece of meat from a lion's cage after they have forgotten to buy some. Thinking the youngster is an orphan, they take him to their kitchen to feed him. Prince Saul arrives at the dinner party, apologising for the King's absence, not knowing his plan has failed, and that his nephew is under the table trying to teach Stan some etiquette whilst he is serving. The dinner party turns into a disaster after Ollie nearly poisons everyone with the soup, and is then unable to carve his speciality, "steak-à-la-Oliver," as the meat stolen from the lion proves too tough. The boys are fired for the foul up, and along with their new friend, spend the night at a mission. A $1,000 reward is posted for the King's return and when one of the mission's down-and-outs recognises him from a photo in the newspaper, the police are alerted and the boys arrested. Prince Saul then plans to poison the King at a reception he is holding for the visiting Prince Prentiloff. Having already tasted Ollie's culinary delights, Saul has the boys released from prison and employs them at the reception so they can be blamed for his dirty work. Stan and Ollie learn of their friends true identity, and unwittingly scupper Saul's plans when they mix up the poisoned salad intended for the King. The King overhears his uncle planning his death so asks Stan and Ollie for help. Saul orders the three out onto the window ledge high above the streets, and they are about to jump when Saul eats an hors d'oeuvre now containing the poison and all are saved with the arrival of the police.

If there was ever a film that proved that the studio executives knew nothing about producing a true Laurel and Hardy film, then this was it. Despite having a proficient comedy director in the chair (Sam Taylor had previously worked with Harold Lloyd) and gag writers including Buster Keaton, the aptly titled NOTHING BUT TROUBLE was easily one of their worst films. Even the use of a witty opening title card, a throwback to the early Roach days, did little to endear it to an already disillusioned public. Almost thankfully, it was their last film for MGM.

THE BULLFIGHTERS

Directed by **Malcolm St. Clair**, Produced by **William Girard**, Edited by **Stanley Rabjohn**, Filmed - Nov/Dec 1944, Released - May 18, 1945 by 20th Century Fox, Running time - 69 minutes.

With: **Richard Lane** ("Hotshot" Coleman), **Carol Andrews** (Hattie Blake/Larceny Nell), **Ralph Sanford** (Richard K. Muldoon), **Edward Gargan** (Bricklayers delegate), **Diosa Costello** (Senorita Conchita), **Irving Gump** (Mr. Gump), **Hank Worden** (Mr. McCoy), **Margo Woode** (Senorita Tangerine), **Jay Novello** (Proprietor of Cafe El Toro, Louis), **Ralph Platz** (Pancho).

Also appeared: Rory Calhoun, Emmett Vogan, Max Wagner, Gus Glassmire, Raphael Storm.

Private detectives Laurel and Hardy arrive in Mexico City hot on the trail of wanted criminal Hattie Blake (nicknamed Larceny Nell) and book in to the Hotel Matador where she is residing. In the city, Richard "Hotshot" Coleman is busily promoting the forthcoming arrival of Don Sebastian, the world's greatest bullfighter from Barcelona. The sports promoter, Richard K. Muldoon nearly dies from shock when he sees a photograph of the matador, as he is the exact double of Stan, whose evidence had put Muldoon behind bars eight years earlier. Even though he was later exonerated, he promises to "skin alive" the

Their Final Reel

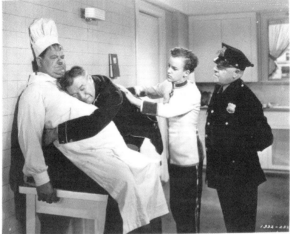

(Top) David Leland (second right) as the exiled King of Orlandia in NOTHING BUT TROUBLE, and below Ollie becomes a target for Esther Howard in THE BIG NOISE

boys if he ever catches up with them. At the hotel Stan is enjoying celebrity status, with the local senoritas also mistaking him for the famous bullfighter. "Hotshot" bumps into Stan and when he realises he is not Don Sebastian, he advises him and Ollie to leave as soon as possible if they value their skins. The boys find Hattie Blake at the cocktail bar but she evades capture after a set-to involving a bowl of eggs. "Hotshot" in the meantime learns that Don Sebastian has been delayed in Spain, so blackmails Stan into impersonating his lookalike until his arrival, threatening to shop them to Muldoon if he refuses. He takes the boys to the Cafe El Toro with Stan now attired as the matador, who receives a great ovation when introduced to the diners. Muldoon and "Hotshot" sign a deal for the bullfight, with Muldoon convinced that Stan is the genuine article. Ollie hides in a phone booth which topples over and knocks Muldoon out cold. On the day of the bullfight, Stan drinks too much "Dutch courage" and wanders off in a drunken daze. The real Don Sebastian turns up and easily tames a murderous bull much to the delight of his adoring fans, while Ollie looks on hardly believing his own eyes. Only when Stan also staggers into the ring does the penny drop, with Muldoon watching from the stands, realising that this is the moment he has been waiting for after all these years. The bulls are let loose in the arena, and during the pandemonium that follows, the boys escape disguised as senoritas. They are packing their bags when Muldoon catches up with them in their hotel room and armed with his knife, carries out his promise.

THE BULLFIGHTERS was Stan and Ollie's final film for 20th Century-Fox after they refused to sign another contract, as they were deeply distressed by the poor content and standard of their films being churned out by the studio. Like others before, it plodded on relying on old Laurel and Hardy material. **HOLLYWOOD PARTY** one of the pictures plundered, with Carol Andrews replacing Lupe Velez in the re-hashed version of the egg breaking routine. As their film careers were all but over, the boys put all efforts into working on the European stage doing the *Driver's Licence* sketch, which proved a big success due partly to a major revival in the screening of old Laurel and Hardy films. Stan's career had now turned full circle. They also made an appearance in the 1947 Royal Command Performance at the London Palladium. The 1947 mini-tour stretched to almost twelve months, before the boys returned to the States in January 1948, exhausted but content in the knowledge that they were still adored in Europe. Ollie made a return to the screen in 1949 appearing as John Wayne's side-kick, Willie Payne, in THE FIGHTING KENTUCKIAN* and again in Frank Capra's RIDING HIGH starring Bing Crosby. Then in 1950, the boys were approached to make another film in France, a multi-national venture with healthy backing from the French government with Stan promised a big say on general production. What should have been a stepping stone to an exciting new future, proved only to be a sad swansong to their movie careers.

*Ollie appeared in the opening titles listed as a co-star along with Vera Ralston and Philip Dorn. The John Wayne Production was written and directed by George Waggner.

ATOLL K

Directed by **Leo Joannon and John Berry** (not credited), Produced by **Raymond Eger**, Edited by **Raymond Isnardon**, Filmed -Aug 1950 - Mar 1951, Released - Nov 21, 1951 by Les Films Sirius, Running time - 98 minutes.

With: **Suzy Delair** (Cherie Lamour), **Max Elloy** (Antoine), **Adriano Rimoldi** (Giovanni Copini), **Luigi Tosi** (Lieutenant Frazer), **Robert Murzeau** (Dolan), **Michael Dalmatoff** (Alecto), **Felix Oudart** (Mayor).

Also appeared: Suzet Mais, Charles Lemontier, Simone Voisin, Robert Vattier, Jean Verner, (Paul Frees is the narrator in the British and American release).

Stan is the heir to his uncle's estate, inheriting a yacht named *Momus* and a South Sea island. He and Ollie arrive in Marseille and set sail for their new home, accompanied by Antoine, a homeless immigrant who acts as their cook, and Giovanni, an out-of-work stonemason. When a storm blows up, the yacht is beached on a newly formed atoll. They quickly adapt to their new life, with the help of a book they find on Robinson Crusoe, and are soon joined on their island by Cherie Lamour, a singer who has run away from her fiancé following an argument at their wedding ceremony. The boys and their friends become smitten with the new arrival and fall over each other trying to win her heart. Cherie's fiancé, Lieutenant Jack Frazer, meets up with her again, after finding the uncharted island whilst working for the navy, and soon discovers that the new atoll is a floating treasure trove loaded with uranium. When nobody can decide who owns the sovereignty to the island, Ollie forms a government and becomes president of "Crusoeland," banning all taxes and rules as part of the constitution. The word soon gets around about the island paradise and it's non-existent laws, and it isn't long before the place is swamped by fortune-seekers. An uprising overthrows Ollie and his government and they are all sentenced to be hanged. As the deed is about to be carried out, another storm blows up and the atoll sinks. The boys, along with Cherie, Antoine and Giovanni are left drifting on the ocean clinging to the gallows, eventually being rescued by Cherie's fiancé. The happy couple finally make it to the altar, Giovanni returns to Italy building fences and Antoine is eaten by a lion while trying to smuggle himself ashore. As for Stan and Ollie, they arrive at their South Sea island, but their idyllic lifestyle is short-lived as the island is confiscated along with all their belongings for non-payment of inheritance tax, and once again the boys find themselves in another nice mess.

The boys' final film can only be described as a complete shambles, with the French and Italian writers unable to speak English. The same went for the actors, who had their voices dubbed, while only Stan and Ollie spoke in English. What should have taken twelve weeks to shoot actually took twelve months (Stan and Ollie both fell ill on the set, which was evident when the film was finally released). Perhaps the only saving grace was that its producers did not resort to cramming it full of old Laurel and Hardy material, as had been done in previous Fox/MGM releases. An 82 minute version was released in Britain in 1952 called ROBINSON CRUSOELAND. The film was finally released in the US in 1954, under the title UTOPIA, again running for 82 minutes.

The Finishing Touch(es)

The Solo Films
Classic Sketches
The British Tours 1947, 1952 & 1953/4
The Final Curtain
The Laurel and Hardy Film Checklist
Sons of the Desert Constitution

THE SOLO FILMS

What Was The Film When..?

THE SOLO FILMS OF STAN LAUREL AND OLIVER HARDY

Oliver Hardy

(Release dates in brackets)
(Bold directed by Stan Laurel)

LUBIN FILM COMPANY

Outwitting Dad (1914), Casey's Birthday (1914), Building A Fire (1914), He Won A Ranch (1914), For Two Pins (1914), The Particular Cowboys (1914), A Tango Tragedy (1914), A Brewerytown Romance (1914), The Female Cop (1914), Good Cider (1914), Long May It Wave (1914), His Sudden Recovery (1914), Who's Boss (1914), The Kidnapped Bride (1914), Worms Will Turn (1914), The Rise Of The Johnsons (1914), He Wanted Work (1914), They Bought A Boat (1914), Back To The Farm (1914), Making Auntie Welcome (1914), The Green Alarm (1914), Never Too Old (1914), A Fool There Was (1914), Pins Are Lucky (1914), Jealous James (1914), When The Ham Turned (1914), The Smuggler's Daughter (1914), She Married For Love (1914), The Soubrette And The Simp (1914), The Honor Of The Force (1914), Kidnapping The Kid (1914), She Was The Other (1914), The Daddy Of Them All (1914), Mother's Baby Boy (1914), The Servant Girl's Legacy (1914), He Wanted His Pants (1914), Dobs At The Shore (1914), The Fresh Air Cure (1914), Weary Willie's Rags (1914), What He Forgot (1915), They Looked Alike (1915), Spaghetti And Lottery (1915), Gus And The Anarchists (1915), Cupid's Target (1915), Shoddy The Tailor (1915), The Prize Baby (1915), An Expensive Visit (1915), Cleaning Time (1915), Mixed Flats (1915), Safety Worst (1915), The Twin Sister (1915), Who Stole The Doggies? (1915), A Lucky Strike (1915), Matilda's Legacy (1915),

Capturing Bad Bill (1915), Her Choice (1915), Cannibal King (1915), What A Cinch (1915), The Dead Letter (1915), Avenging Bill (1915), The Haunted Hat (1915), Babe's School Days (1915), Edison Bugg's Invention (1916), A Terrible Tragedy (1916), It Happened In Pikersville (1916).

EDISON FILM COMPANY

It May Be You (1915), Not Much Force (1915), Poor Baby (1915), Clothes Makes The Man (1915), The Simp And The Sophomores (1915).

WHARTON BROTHERS

The Bungalow Bungle* (1915), Three Rings And A Goat* (1915), A Rheumatic Joint* (1915), The Lilac Splash* (1915). *Episodes 1,2,3 & 5 of the serial New Adventures of J. Rufus Wallingford.

CASINO STAR

Ethel's Romeos (1915).

STARLIGHT

Fatty's Fatal Fun (1915).

NOVELTY

Something In Her Eye (1915), A Janitor's Joyful Job (1915).

WIZARD COMEDIES

The Crazy Clock Maker (1915).

VIM COMEDIES

The Midnight Prowlers (1915), Pressing Business (1915), Love Pepper And Sweets (1915), Strangled Harmony (1915), Speed Kings (1915), Mixed And Fixed (1915), Ups And Downs (1915), This Way Out (1916), Chickens (1916), Frenzied Finance (1916), Busted Hearts (1916), A Sticky Affair (1916), Bungles' Rainy Day (1916), One Too Many (1916), Bungles Enforces The Law (1916), The Serenade (1916), Bungles' Elopement (1916), Nerve And

What Was The Film When..?

Gasoline (1916), Bungles Lands A Job (1916), Their Vacation (1916), Mamma's Boys (1916), The Battle Royal (1916), All For A Girl (1916), Hired And Fired (1916), What's Sauce For The Goose (1916), The Brave Ones (1916), The Water Cure (1916), Thirty Days (1916), Baby Doll (1916), The Schemers (1916), Sea Dogs (1916), Hungry Hearts (1916), Never Again (1916), Better Halves (1916), A Day At School (1916), Spaghetti (1916), Aunt Bill (1916), The Heroes (1916), Human Hounds (1916), Dreamy Knights (1916), Life Savers (1916), Their Honeymoon (1916), The Tryout (1916), An Aerial Joyride (1916), Sidetracked (1916), Stranded (1916), Love And Duty (1916), The Reformers (1916), Royal Blood (1916), The Candy Trail (1916), The Precious Parcel (1916), A Maid To Order (1916), Twin Flats (1916), A Warm Reception (1916), Pipe Dreams (1916), Mother's Child (1916), Prize Winners (1916), The Guilty Ones (1916), He Winked And Won (1916), Fat And Fickle (1916), The Boycotted Baby (1917), The Other Girl (1917), The Love Bugs (1917), A Mix Up In Hearts (1917), Wanted - A Bad Man (1917).

F. RAY COMSTOCK PHOTO COMPANY

The Lottery Man (1916).

KING BEE

Back Stage (1917), The Hero (1917), Dough-Nuts (1917), Cupid's Rival (1917), The Villain (1917), The Millionaire (1917), The Goat (1917), The Fly Cop (1917), The Chief Cook (1917), The Candy Kid (1917), The Hobo (1917), The Pest (1917), The Band Master (1917), The Slave (1917), The Stranger (1918), His Day Out (1918), The Rogue (1918), The Orderly (1918), The Scholar (1918), The Messenger (1918), The Handy Man (1918), The Straight And Narrow (1918), Playmates (1918), Beauties In Distress (1918).

REELCRAFT PICTURES

Married To Order (1920), Distilled Love (1920).

L-KO STUDIOS

Business Before Honesty (1918), Hello Trouble (1918), Painless Love (1918), The King Of The Kitchen (1918), The Freckled Fish (1919), Hop The Bellhop (1919), Lions And Ladies (1919), Hearts And Hocks (1919).

VITAGRAPH

Soapsuds And Sapheads (1919), Jazz And Jailbirds (1919), Mules And Mortgages (1919), Tootsies and Tamales (1919), Healthy And Happy (1919), Flips And Flops (1919), Yaps And Yokels (1919), Dull Care (1919), Mates And Models (1919), Squabs And Squabbles (1919), The Head Waiter (1919), Switches And Sweeties (1919), Bungs And Bunglers (1919), Dames And Dentists (1920), Maids And Muslin (1920), Squeaks And Squawks (1920), Fists And Fodder (1920), Pals And Pugs (1920), He Laughs Last (1920), Springtime (1920), The Decorator (1920), The Stage Hand (1920), The Backyard (1920), His Jonah Day (1920), The Trouble Hunter (1920), The Nuisance (1921), The Mysterious Stranger (1920), The Blizzard (1921), The Tourist (1921), The Rent Collector (1921), The Bakery (1921), The Fall Guy (1921), The Bellhop (1921), The Sawmill (1922), The Show (1922), Quicksands (1923), A Pair Of Kings (1922), Fortune's Mask (1922), The Little Wildcat (1922), Golf (1922), The Agent (1922), The Counter Jumper (1922), No Wedding Bells (1923), The Barnyard (1923), The Midnight Cabaret (1923), The Gown Shop (1923), Lightning Love (1923), Horseshoes (1923), Trouble Brewing (1924).

CHADWICK PICTURES

The Girl In The Limousine (1924), Her Boyfriend (1924), Kid Speed (1924), The Wizard Of Oz (1925), The Perfect Clown (1925).

ARROW PICTURES

Stick Around (1925), Rivals (1925), Hey, Taxi! (1925), Fiddlin' Around (1925), Hop To It! (1925), The Joke's On You (1925), They All Fall (1925).

HAL ROACH STUDIOS

Wild Papa (1924), Isn't Life Terrible (1925), Should Sailors Marry? (1925), **Yes Yes Nanette (1925), Wandering Papas (1926),** Laughing Ladies (1925), **Madame Mystery (1926),** Say It With Babies (1926), Long Fliv The King (1926), Thundering Fleas (1926), Along Came Auntie (1926), Two Time Mama (1927), Bromo And Juliet (1926), Crazy Like A Fox (1926), Galloping Ghosts

(1928), Be Your Age (1926), The Nickel Hopper (1926), Why Girls Say No (1927), Honorable Mr. Buggs (1927), Should Men Walk Home? (1927), No Man's Law (1927), Fluttering Hearts (1927), Baby Brother (1927), Love 'Em And Feed 'Em (1927), Barnum And Ringling, Inc. (1928), Zenobia (1939).

FOX STUDIOS
Neptune's Stepdaughter (1925), The Gentle Cyclone (1926), A Bankrupt Honeymoon (1926).

LARRY SEMON PRODUCTIONS
Stop, Look and Listen (1926).

MACK SENNETT
Crazy To Act (1927).

JOHN WAYNE PRODUCTIONS
The Fighting Kentuckian (1949).

PARAMOUNT PICTURES
Riding High (1950).

The Finishing Touch(es)

Stan Laurel

(Release dates in brackets)

BERNSTEIN PRODUCTIONS
Nuts In May (c1917).

UNIVERSAL, NESTOR AND L-KO
Phoney Photos (1918), Hickory Hiram (1918), Whose Zoo (1918), O It's Great To Be Crazy (1918).

ROLIN
Do You Love Your Wife? (1919), Just Rambling Along (1918), Hoot Mon! (1919), No Place Like Jail (1918), Hustling For Health (1919).

VITAGRAPH
Huns And Hyphens (1918), Bears And Bad Men (1918), Frauds And Frenzies (1918).

METRO PICTURES
A Weak-End Party (1922), The Handy Man (1923), The Egg (1922), The Pest (1922), Mud And Sand (1922), When Knights Were Cold (1923).

SAMUEL BISCHOFF
Mixed Nuts (1925).

HAL ROACH STUDIOS
Under Two Jags (1923), The Noon Whistle (1923), White Wings (1923), Pick And Shovel (1923), Kill or Cure (1923), Collars And Cuffs (1923), Gas And Air (1923), Oranges And Lemons (1923), Short Orders (1923), Save The Ship (1923), A Man About Town (1923), Roughest Africa (1923), Scorching Sands (1923), The Whole Truth (1923), Frozen Hearts (1923), The Soilers (1923), Mother's Joy (1923), Near Dublin (1924), Smithy (1924), Zeb Vs. Paprika (1924), Postage Due (1924), Brothers Under The Chin (1924), Wide Open Spaces (1924), Rupert Of Hee Haw (1924),

Short Kilts (1924), What's The World Coming To? (1926), Get 'Em Young (1926), On The Front Page (1926), Seeing The World (1927), Eve's Love Letters (1927), Should Tall Men Marry? (1928).

JOE ROCK

Detained (1924), Mandarin Mix-Up (1924), Monsieur Don't Care (1924), West Of Hot Dog (1924), Somewhere In Wrong (1925), Twins (1925), Pie-Eyed (1925), The Snow Hawk (1925), Navy Blue Days (1925), The Sleuth (1925), Dr. Pyckle And Mr. Pride (1925), Half A Man (1925).

For further information on the solo films of Laurel and Hardy see *Laurel or Hardy* by Rob Stone.

CLASSIC SKETCHES

'Why don't we become bandits.'
The Prison schoolroom scene
'Soda...soda...soda...'
The furniture payment?
Stan and Mrs Bickerdyke

What Was The Film When..?

Classic Sketches

(Authors choice)

FRA DIAVOLO - 'Why don't we become bandits?'
The boys have just been robbed of their life savings.

(Ollio)	'There it goes. After all we went through to get it.'
(Stanlio)	'Oh well, come easy go easy, that's my motto.'
(Ollio)	'What do you mean come easy, go easy? Now we've got to start all over again right at the bottom.'
(Stanlio)	'Why don't we start at the top?'
(Ollio)	'What do you mean?'
(Stanlio)	'Why don't we become bandits? Then we wouldn't have to work hard anymore. Let's get it the easy way. We could rob the rich and give 'em to the poor and we could...'
(Ollio)	'That's the first time that you've shown any intelligence.'
(Stanlio)	'Well it's the first time you've listened to me. You know, if you'd listen to me once in a while you'd be a lot better off.'
(Ollio)	'I guess you're right...tell me that plan again.'
(Stanlio)	'All of it?'
(Ollio)	'Certainly, certainly.'
(Stanlio)	'Well, if we became rich and, and we robbed the poor and we gave em to the bandits...we could start at the top and we could get to the bottom without working hard anymore...we can't go wrong, it's the law of conversation.'
(Ollio)	'What do you mean?'
(Stanlio)	'Well, as you cast your bread on the waters...so shall ye reap.'
(Ollio)	'That's very well thought out.'
(Stanlio)	'I'm glad you agree.'
(Ollio)	'Mmm.'
(Stanlio)	'You know, there's one thing that's bothering me though.'

(Ollio)	'What's that?'
(Stanlio)	'We don't know anything about being bandits. I never...'
(Ollio)	'Why it's simple. We can be bandits. It doesn't require any brains!'

PARDON US – The Prison Schoolroom Scene

(Fin)	'We shall now have an intelligence test. Who was Columbus?'
(Con)	'The mayor of Ohio.'
(Fin)	'What did he do?'
(Con)	'He died.'
(Fin)	'Of course he died. Who killed him?'
(Mugsie)	'Cock Robin.'
(Fin)	'Who said that?'
(Mugsie)	'I did!'
(Fin)	'Correct.'
(Fin)	'What is a blizzard?'
(Stan)	'A blizzard…a blizzard is the inside of a buzzard.'
(Fin)	'Hmm, fresh huh.'
(Fin)	'How many times do 3 go into 9?'
(Stan)	'Three times.'
(Fin)	'Correct.'
(Stan)	'And two left over.'
(Fin)	*(to Ollie)* 'What are you laughing at?'
(Ollie)	'There's only one left over.'
(Fin)	'Doh!'
(Fin)	'Listen, you spell needle.'
(Ollie)	'N-E-I-D-L-E.'
(Fin)	'There is no I in needle.'
(Stan)	'Then it's a rotten needle!'
	(Ball of paper then hits Fin on the head)
(Fin)	'Who did that? If I find out who did it, they'll stand in the corner.' *(groans from the class of cons)*
(Fin)	'Now. What is a comet? You.'
(Con)	'A comet…a comet is a star with a tail on it.'

(Fin)	'Right…name one?'
(Stan)	'Rin Tin Tin.'
(Fin)	'Doh…just for that you'll stay after school.'

MEN O'WAR – 'Soda...Soda...Soda...'

(Girlfriend)	'I don't know what I want.' *(Stan knocks on window)*
(Ollie)	'Pardon me, just a moment, be right back' *(exits)*
(Ollie)	'Just how big is this bankroll…15 cents. Is that all you've got?'
(Stan)	'I lost the rest.'
(Ollie)	'Well that won't buy four drinks.'
(Stan)	'What'll we do?'
(Ollie)	'I have an idea. When I ask you to have a drink, you refuse.' *(Re-enters)*
(Ollie)	'Everything is just going to be fine. Soda, soda, soda, and what will you have Stan?'
(Stan)	'Soda.'
(Ollie)	'Pardon me.' *(Stan and Ollie exit)*
(Ollie)	'Don't you understand we've only got 15 cents? Now when I ask you to have a drink, you refuse. Do you understand?' *(Stan and Ollie return)*
(Ollie)	'Soda, soda, soda, and what will you have Stan?'
(Stan)	'Soda.'
(Ollie)	'Just a moment please, pardon me, once more.' *(They go outside where Ollie hits Stan, and Stan pinches Ollie's chest)*
(Ollie)	'Can't you grasp the situation? You must refuse.'
(Stan)	'But you keep asking me.'
(Ollie)	'I'm only putting it on for the girls.'
(Stan)	'Ohhh.'
(Ollie)	'And we've only got 15 cents.'
(Ollie)	'That's it, now come on.' *(Stan and Ollie return)*
(Ollie)	'Now let's see. Soda, soda, and just soda, and my dear Stan, what will you have?'
(Stan)	'I don't want any.'
(Girlfriend)	'Oh general, don't be a piker.'

The Finishing Touch(es)

(Stan)	'All right, I'll have a banana split.'
(Ollie)	'Pardon me just a moment.' (*kicks Stan, Stan kicks him back.*)
(Ollie)	'Don't do that' (*pushes Stan. Stan pokes him in eye.*)
(Ollie)	'Just playing together.' (*pinches Stan*)
(Ollie)	'Three sodas (*whispers to Stan*) we can split ours.'
(Fin)	'And er, what flavour please?'
(Girlfriend)	'Cherry.'
(Fin)	'OK yes and you?'
(Other Girlfriend)	'Chocolate.'
(Fin)	'Chocolate hm hm, and yours?'
(Ollie)	(*shyly*) 'Sassafras (*Stan taps him*) what is it now?'
(Stan)	'I don't like Frassasas.'
(Fin)	'Doh.'
(Ollie)	'Three sodas. One with frassas…sassafras.'
(Ollie)	'And shut up.' (*speaking to Stan*)
(Fin)	'Sassafras.'
(Ollie)	'Go ahead and drink your half.' (*Stan drains glass*)
(Ollie)	'Do you know what you've done? What made you do it?'
(Stan)	'I couldn't help it.'
(Ollie)	'Why?'
(Stan)	'My half was on the bottom!'
(Ollie)	'Gimme a cheque.' (*cheque reads 30 cents*)
(Ollie)	'That's all right Stan. I'm not a bit mad. It's your party and I'm gonna let you pay the cheque.'
(Stan)	'You're not mad at me?'
(Ollie)	'Not a bit. Come ladies.' (*Stan looks at bill, plays the fruit machine and wins the jackpot*)

THICKER THAN WATER - The Furniture Payment?

(Mrs Hardy)	'Oh, good afternoon Mr. Finlayson.'
(Fin)	'Good afternoon.'
(Mrs Hardy)	'What's the idea?'
(Fin)	'I'm here to collect the payment on the furniture.'

(Mrs Hardy)	'Why it was paid yesterday.'
(Fin)	'Steady woman, not to me it wasn't.'
(Mrs Hardy)	'Oliver...Oliver.'
(Ollie)	'Yes baby I'm coming.'
(Mrs Hardy)	'There must be some mistake...Oliver, did I or did I not give you the money to pay on the furniture?'
(Ollie)	'You certainly did.'
(Mrs Hardy)	'Then why wasn't it paid?'
(Ollie)	'Why I gave it to him to pay it for me.'
(Mrs Hardy)	'Then what did you do with it?'
(Stan)	'I gave it back to him.'
(Ollie)	'You gave it to me?'
(Stan)	'Yeh, I gave it to you to pay my room and board. Then you gave it to her. Recomember?'
(Mrs Hardy)	'Do you mean to say that the money that he gave to you, that you gave to him, that he gave to me, was the same money that I gave to him to pay him?'
(Stan)	'Well if that was the money that you gave to him, to give to me, to pay to him, it must have been the money that I gave him, to give to you to pay my rent, didn't I?'
(Mrs Hardy)	'Mr. Finlayson, I owe you an apology.'
(Fin)	'And thirty seven dollars.'
(Mrs Hardy)	'Then this money must belong to you.'
(Fin)	'And the next time I want my payment without any detour. Huh...he gave it to you, and you gave it to him, and who gave it to what. Why you're all nuts.'
(Mrs Hardy)	'You big dumb-bell, I can't trust you to do a thing, and as for you, I've a good mind to throw you out.'
(Stan)	'You can't do it.'
(Mrs Hardy)	'I can't do it?'
(Stan)	'No, because I've paid my room and board in advance, and I gave it to him.'
(Ollie)	'What do you mean, you gave it to me, that was the money that she gave to me, and I gave it to you, to give to him, then you gave it back to me and I had to

	give it to her to give to him.'
(Stan)	'Was that the money that she gave to him that I gave to you to give to...'
(Ollie)	'Why certainly.'
(Stan)	'Well if she wants to give it to him, that's her business. No use you and I arguing about it.'
(Mrs Hardy)	'Oh cut it out, cut it out.'

BONNIE SCOTLAND - Stan and Mrs Bickerdyke

(Mrs Bickerdyke)	'Good morning Mr. McLaurel.'
(Stan)	'Good morning Mrs. Bickerdyke.'
(Mrs Bickerdyke)	'Where is Mr. Hardy, I haven't seen him in the past three weeks?'
(Stan)	'Oh, he's awful sick.'
(Mrs Bickerdyke)	'Is that a fact?'
(Stan)	'Hoot mon. You know the day he fell in the water, he got an awful cold...and it turned into pneumatics.'
(Mrs Bickerdyke)	'Is he very sick?'
(Stan)	'You're darn hootin he's sick. You know the only thing he can keep on his stomach is a hot water bottle.'
(Mrs Bickerdyke)	'My, my, what a predicament.'
(Stan)	'Yeh, I think he's got that too.'

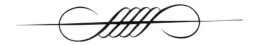

Dennis King as the bandit leader in FRA DIAVOLO (THE DEVIL'S BROTHER)

THE BRITISH TOURS
1947 - The Driver's Licence Sketch
1952 - A Spot of Trouble
1953/54 - Birds of a Feather

What Was The Film When..?
THE BRITISH TOURS

1947 – "The Driver's Licence Sketch"
Tour dates (from) and venues

Feb 24	NEWCASTLE Empire
Mar 3	BIRMINGHAM Hippodrome
Mar 10	LONDON Palladium
Mar 31	LONDON Wimbledon
Apr 7	LEWISHAM Hippodrome
Apr 14	LONDON Coliseum
Apr 27	LONDON Victoria Palace
May 12	DUDLEY Hippodrome
May 19	LIVERPOOL Empire
May 26	MORECAMBE Victoria Pavilion
Jun 2	BLACKPOOL Palace
Jun 9	GLASGOW Empire
Jun 23	SKEGNESS Butlin's
Jun 30	EDINBURGH Empire
Jul 7	HULL New Theatre
Jul 14	BRISTOL Hippodrome
Jul 21	MANCHESTER Palace
Aug 4	SOUTHSEA King's
Aug 11	BOSCOMBE Hippodrome
Aug 18	MARGATE Winter Gardens
Aug 25	COVENTRY Hippodrome
Sep 8	BOLTON Lido
Sep 15	SWINDON Empire
Sep 22	FINSBURY PARK Empire & CHISWICK Empire
Nov 3	LONDON Palladium (Royal Variety Performance)

1952 – "A Spot of Trouble" (Or "On The Spot")
Tour dates (from) and venues

Feb 25	PETERBOROUGH Embassy
Mar 10	GLASGOW Empire
Mar 16	NORTH SHIELDS Gaumont Cinema
Mar 17	NEWCASTLE Empire
Mar 24	SUNDERLAND Empire

The Finishing Touch(es)

Mar 31	HANLEY Royal
Apr 7	LEEDS Empire
Apr 14	NOTTINGHAM Empire
Apr 21	SHREWSBURY Granada
Apr 28	EDINBURGH Empire
May 5	BIRMINGHAM Hippodrome
May 12	SOUTHAMPTON Gaumont
May 19	LIVERPOOL Empire
May 27	DUBLIN Olympia
Jun 9	BELFAST Grand Opera House
Jun 30	SHEFFIELD Empire
Jul 7	BRIGHTON Hippodrome
Jul 14	MANCHESTER Palace
Jul 21	RHYL Queen's
Jul 28	BRADFORD Alhambra
Aug 4	SOUTHEND Odeon
Aug 11	COVENTRY Hippodrome
Aug 18	SOUTHPORT Garrick
Aug 25	SUTTON Granada
Sep 1	BRISTOL Hippodrome
Sep 5	CLIFTON Grand Spa Hotel
Sep 8	PORTSMOUTH Royal
Sep 15	DUDLEY Hippodrome
Sep 22	SWANSEA Empire
Sep 29	CARDIFF New Theatre

1953-54 – "Birds of a Feather"
Tour dates (from) and venues

Oct 11	DUBLIN Olympia
Oct 19	NORTHAMPTON New Theatre
Oct 26	LIVERPOOL Empire
Nov 2	MANCHESTER Hippodrome
Nov 9	FINSBURY PARK Empire*
Nov 16	BRIXTON Empress
Nov 23	NEWCASTLE Empire
Nov 30	BIRMINGHAM Hippodrome
Dec 7	HULL Palace
Dec 21	NOTTINGHAM Empire

What Was The Film When..?

1954

Jan 18	PORTSMOUTH Royal
Jan 25	CHISWICK Empire
Feb 1	FINSBURY PARK Empire
Feb 8	BRIGHTON Hippodrome
Feb 15	NORWICH Hippodrome
Feb 22	SUNDERLAND Empire
Mar 1	GLASGOW Empire
Mar 8	WOLVERHAMPTON Hippodrome
Mar 15	SHEFFIELD Empire
Mar 22	YORK Empire
Mar 29	GRIMSBY Palace
Apr 5	LEEDS Empire
Apr 12	EDINBURGH Empire
Apr 19	CARLISLE Her Majesty's
May 3	BRADFORD Alhambra
May 10	ASTON Hippodrome
May 17	PLYMOUTH Palace

*Stan and Ollie did not perform due to illness.

For further information please see *Laurel and Hardy, The British Tours* by A. J. Marriot.

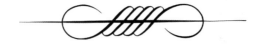

The Finishing Touch(es)

THE FINAL CURTAIN

After completing ATOLL K, the boys were content to do nothing more than recover from the illness endured during filming. In 1952 both Stan and Ollie were fit enough to resume work, and they set out on their second tour of the British Isles, with a newly written sketch entitled *A Spot Of Trouble* based loosely on the 1930 short NIGHT OWLS. Again the boys were welcomed with open arms by an adoring crowd, so it was no surprise when they toured again in 1953 performing *Birds Of A Feather* playing to packed houses and mobbed wherever they appeared.

Then at the end of 1954, they made a surprise return to the screen, when they unwittingly starred on the television programme *This Is Your Life*. Their popularity continued to soar with the showing of their films on television and they were persuaded to work again. Just as they were about to begin, Ollie fell ill. Never really recovering, he died in the early hours of August 7, 1957. Stan was heartbroken, but because of his own health problems, was forbidden by his doctor from attending the funeral. Laurel and Hardy were no more. Stan spent his time replying to the huge amounts of fan mail he constantly received, as well as writing new material. He also enjoyed entertaining at his Santa Monica home, with both film stars and fans welcomed. In 1961 he was awarded an honorary Oscar for his contribution to movies, which pleased him greatly, except that his old buddy was not there to share in the glory. Stan continued to answer his ever growing pile of fan mail on his trusty typewriter, until in the small hours of February 23, 1965, he told his last joke and died peacefully.

John McCabe, Al Kilgore and others formed a Laurel and Hardy Appreciation Society called "Sons Of The Desert," a fan club openly encouraged by Stan when he was alive. There are now thousands of devoted "Sons" all over the world, meeting regularly to watch the films and talk about their idols. Al Kilgore designed an escutcheon, with the Latin inscription at the bottom of the design translating as "Two minds without a single thought."

It's now more than half a century since their last film, but it is a testimony to their undying popularity that all over the world, peals of laughter can still be heard whenever one of their films has a showing. They were unique. We shall never see their like again.

What Was The Film When..?
LAUREL & HARDY FILM CHECKLIST

Film	VHS	DVD	8/16mm	Seen
The Lucky Dog	☐	☐	☐	☐
45 Minutes From Hollywood	☐	☐	☐	☐
Duck Soup	☐	☐	☐	☐
Slipping Wives	☐	☐	☐	☐
Love 'Em And Weep	☐	☐	☐	☐
Why Girls Love Sailors	☐	☐	☐	☐
With Love And Hisses	☐	☐	☐	☐
Sailors, Beware!	☐	☐	☐	☐
Now I'll Tell One	☐	☐	☐	☐
Do Detectives Think?	☐	☐	☐	☐
Flying Elephants	☐	☐	☐	☐
Sugar Daddies	☐	☐	☐	☐
The Second Hundred Years	☐	☐	☐	☐
Call Of The Cuckoos	☐	☐	☐	☐
Hats Off	☐	☐	☐	☐
Putting Pants On Philip	☐	☐	☐	☐
The Battle Of The Century	☐	☐	☐	☐
Leave 'Em Laughing	☐	☐	☐	☐
The Finishing Touch	☐	☐	☐	☐
From Soup To Nuts	☐	☐	☐	☐
You're Darn Tootin'	☐	☐	☐	☐
Their Purple Moment	☐	☐	☐	☐
Should Married Men Go Home?	☐	☐	☐	☐
Early To Bed	☐	☐	☐	☐
Two Tars	☐	☐	☐	☐
Habeas Corpus	☐	☐	☐	☐
We Faw Down	☐	☐	☐	☐
Liberty	☐	☐	☐	☐
Wrong Again	☐	☐	☐	☐
That's My Wife	☐	☐	☐	☐
Big Business	☐	☐	☐	☐
Double Whoopee	☐	☐	☐	☐
Bacon Grabbers	☐	☐	☐	☐
Angora Love	☐	☐	☐	☐

The Finishing Touch(es)

Film	VHS	DVD	8/16mm	Seen
Unaccustomed As We Are	☐	☐	☐	☐
Berth Marks	☐	☐	☐	☐
Men O'War	☐	☐	☐	☐
The Hollywood Revue of 1929	☐	☐	☐	☐
Perfect Day	☐	☐	☐	☐
They Go Boom	☐	☐	☐	☐
The Hoose-Gow	☐	☐	☐	☐
The Rogue Song	☐	☐	☐	☐
Night Owls	☐	☐	☐	☐
Blotto	☐	☐	☐	☐
Brats	☐	☐	☐	☐
Below Zero	☐	☐	☐	☐
Hog Wild	☐	☐	☐	☐
The Laurel-Hardy Murder Case	☐	☐	☐	☐
Pardon Us	☐	☐	☐	☐
Another Fine Mess	☐	☐	☐	☐
Be Big	☐	☐	☐	☐
Chickens Come Home	☐	☐	☐	☐
The Stolen Jools	☐	☐	☐	☐
Laughing Gravy	☐	☐	☐	☐
Our Wife	☐	☐	☐	☐
Come Clean	☐	☐	☐	☐
One Good Turn	☐	☐	☐	☐
Beau Hunks	☐	☐	☐	☐
On The Loose	☐	☐	☐	☐
Helpmates	☐	☐	☐	☐
Any Old Port	☐	☐	☐	☐
The Music Box	☐	☐	☐	☐
The Chimp	☐	☐	☐	☐
County Hospital	☐	☐	☐	☐
Pack Up Your Troubles	☐	☐	☐	☐
Scram!	☐	☐	☐	☐
Their First Mistake	☐	☐	☐	☐
Towed In The Hole	☐	☐	☐	☐
Twice Two	☐	☐	☐	☐
Fra Diavolo	☐	☐	☐	☐

What Was The Film When..?

Film	VHS	DVD	8/16mm	Seen
Me And My Pal	☐	☐	☐	☐
The Midnight Patrol	☐	☐	☐	☐
Busy Bodies	☐	☐	☐	☐
Wild Poses	☐	☐	☐	☐
Dirty Work	☐	☐	☐	☐
Sons Of The Desert	☐	☐	☐	☐
Hollywood Party	☐	☐	☐	☐
Oliver The Eighth	☐	☐	☐	☐
Going Bye-Bye!	☐	☐	☐	☐
Them Thar Hills	☐	☐	☐	☐
Babes In Toyland	☐	☐	☐	☐
The Live Ghost	☐	☐	☐	☐
Tit For Tat	☐	☐	☐	☐
The Fixer-Uppers	☐	☐	☐	☐
Bonnie Scotland	☐	☐	☐	☐
Thicker Than Water	☐	☐	☐	☐
The Bohemian Girl	☐	☐	☐	☐
Our Relations	☐	☐	☐	☐
On The Wrong Trek	☐	☐	☐	☐
Way Out West	☐	☐	☐	☐
Pick A Star	☐	☐	☐	☐
Swiss Miss	☐	☐	☐	☐
Block-Heads	☐	☐	☐	☐
A Chump At Oxford	☐	☐	☐	☐
The Flying Deuces	☐	☐	☐	☐
Saps At Sea	☐	☐	☐	☐
Great Guns	☐	☐	☐	☐
A-Haunting We Will Go	☐	☐	☐	☐
Air Raid Wardens	☐	☐	☐	☐
Jitterbugs	☐	☐	☐	☐
The Tree In A Test Tube	☐	☐	☐	☐
The Dancing Masters	☐	☐	☐	☐
The Big Noise	☐	☐	☐	☐
Nothing But Trouble	☐	☐	☐	☐
The Bullfighters	☐	☐	☐	☐
Atoll K	☐	☐	☐	☐

THE SONS OF THE DESERT CONSTITUTION

Article 1. The Sons of the Desert is an organization with scholarly overtones and heavily social undertones devoted to the loving study of the persons and films of Stan Laurel and Oliver Hardy.

Article 2. The founding members are Orson Bean, Al Kilgore, John McCabe, Chuck McCann, and John Municino.

Article 3. The Sons of the Desert shall have the following officers and board members, who will be elected at an annual meeting: Grand Sheik, Vice-Sheik (Sheik in charge of vice), Grand Vizier (Corresponding Secretary), Sub-Vice-Vizier (Treasurer and in charge of sub-vice), Board members-at-large (this number should not exceed 812).

Article 4. All officers and Board members-at large shall sit at an exalted place at the annual banquet table.

Article 5. The officers and Board members-at large shall have absolutely no authority whatever.

Article 6. Despite his absolute lack of authority, the Grand Shiek or his deputy shall act as chairman at all meetings, and will follow the standard parliamentary procedure in conducting same. At the meetings, it is hoped that the innate dignity, sensitivity, and good taste of the members assembled will permit activities to be conducted with a lively sense of deportment and good order.

Article 7. Article 6 is ridiculous.

Article 8. The Annual Meeting shall be conducted in the following sequence:
a. Cocktails
b. Business meeting and cocktails

c. Dinner (with cocktails)
d. After-dinner speeches and cocktails
e. Cocktails
f. Coffee and cocktails
g. Showing of Laurel and Hardy films
h. After-film critique and cocktails
i. After-after-film critique and cocktails
j. Stan has suggested this period. In his words; *'All members are requested to park their camels and hire a taxi; then return for "one for the desert."'*

Article 9. Section "d" from above shall consist in part of the following toasts:
1. "To Stan"
2. "To Babe"
3. "To Fin"
4. "To Mae Busch and Charlie Hall - who are eternally ever-popular."

Article 10. Section "h" above shall include the reading of scholarly papers on Laurel and Hardy. Any member going over an eight and a half minute time limit shall have his cocktails limited to fourteen in number.

Article 11. Hopefully, and seriously, The Sons of the Desert, in the strong desire to perpetuate the spirit and genius of Laurel and Hardy will conduct activities ultimately and always devoted to the preservation of their films and the encouragement of their showing everywhere.

Article 12. There shall be member societies in other cities called "Tents," each of which shall derive its name from one of the films.

Article 13. Stan has suggested that members might wear a fez or blazer patch with an appropriate motto. He says *'I hope that the motto can be blue and gray, showing two derbies with these words superimposed:'* "Two minds without a single thought." These words have been duly set into the delightful escutcheon created for The Sons of the Desert by Al Kilgore. They have been rendered into Latin in the spirit of Stan's dictum that our organization should have, to use his words, a "half-assed dignity" about it. We shall strive to maintain precisely that kind of dignity at all costs - at all times.

The Finishing Touch(es)

Sons of the Desert Song

"WE ARE THE SONS OF THE DESERT,
HAVING THE TIME OF OUR LIVES,
MARCHING ALONG, TWO THOUSAND STRONG,
FAR FROM OUR SWEETHEARTS AND WIVES
GOD BLESS THEM.
TRAMP TRAMP TRAMP
THE BOYS ARE MARCHING,
ATTESTING* TO THIS MELODY
LA LA LA LA LA
LA LA LA LA LA LA LA
SONS OF THE DESERT ARE WE."

(*OR "AND DANCING")

Notes: